On the left, the late George Collins with an old friend at Ramsholt Quay on the river Deben. George was born in 1903 and was employed as chauffeur/boatman at Bawdsey Hall for many years, after which he became full-time harbourmaster at Ramsholt. Always the first to help yachtsmen in difficulties, maker of trawl nets, ferryman across the Deben from Ramsholt to Hemley Hard and at all times in great demand with his host of mardles about the river and its characters, he became a legend in his own lifetime.

Photography: Ronald Cobley

MARDLES FROM SUFFOLK

MARDLES
FROM
SUFFOLK

A taste of
East Anglian humour

Ernest R. Cooper, F. S. A.

COUNTRYSIDE BOOKS
NEWBURY, BERKSHIRE

First Published in 1932
Reprinted by Barbara Hopkinson Books 1984
© Judith Elizabeth Cooper 1984
This edition published 1989

Reprinted 1999

COUNTRYSIDE BOOKS
3 CATHERINE ROAD
NEWBURY, BERKSHIRE

ISBN 1 85306 065 8

Produced through MRM Associates Ltd., Reading
Printed in England by J.W. Arrowsmith Ltd., Bristol

PREFACE

My father, Ernest Read Cooper, was East Anglian born and bred. Throughout his life much of his spare time was devoted to recording many facets of East Anglian life and history. His interests covered a wide range including farm and country life and pursuits, the coast, sailing, the Lifeboat and the Militia, for which he wrote a chapter for the Suffolk Regimental History.

He had a great sense of humour and among his many papers and MSS is a large commonplace book about Woodbridge, Southwold, Dunwich and other localities; it also contains notes on the subjects of ghosts, smugglers and folklore. Every so often a page is turned and the next title is "Fun", under which heading are recorded many stories of East Anglian humour and wit.

This little volume has its fair share of "Fun" culled from his commonplace book. He would have been happy to share it with a new generation.

Judith Elizabeth Cooper

CONTENTS

x CONTENTS

MARDLES FROM SUFFOLK

I

MARDLIN IN THE HALF AND HALFER INN

YEARS ago, when little people had a chance in life, a small class of fishing boat came into vogue, known as Half and Halfers, owing to the arrangement by which the owner took half the proceeds of the voyage, and kept the boat and gear up, and the crew took the other half and doled it in shares among themselves. These boats were fifteen to twenty tons, clinker built, about forty-five feet long, by fifteen feet beam and seven feet depth, with gaff mainsail and lug mizen, sheeted to an outligger, and carried a crew of eight.

Many of these men worked on the land for part of the year, and went the voyages in between, and for some reason they were known as " Peabellies." I recollect, in my early yachting days, my skipper having an exchange of compliments with some of them who nearly ran us down going into Lowestoft.

He, being a real deep water man, replied to their rude words in scornful tones, " You want some more peas in your belly," which from some obscure reason seemed to be a telling retort. I call to mind one of these men, hailing from Blythburgh, whose mother told us what a good boy he was, and " never sent his washing home but what he put some sea-biscuits in the toes of his dirty stockings."

Scores of these little boats were built and worked on the Suffolk coast until they were out-classed, and died out about forty to fifty years ago, but I keep the name alive as the sign of a little quayside beer-house frequented by many of these hardy, cheery, and sometimes beery Suffolk fishermen. Many a funny breeze has been weathered, many tales of marvellous catches, and narrow squeaks at sea, have been told, and retold, within the radius of the antique, high-backed settle, which almost surrounds the old fashioned hob grate.

The grate itself was used at fitting out times to heat the boats' branding irons ; and on the back of the settle can still be seen where the hot irons of various, otherwise long-forgotten craft, were tested by mischievous, half-share, boys, since become grandfathers, and mostly gone their last voyage to the churchyard.

They say on the cliff that if good fishermen and sailormen are wanted again they will have to be dug up out of the graveyard, and yet the Captain of the *Warspite* training Ship, said only the other day that his best boys still come from Suffolk and Norfolk.

All the local gossip, and much of the news of the day, can be gathered in these little pubs when the customers drop in during the forenoon for their " levenses," or after tea when the day's work is done, and weary arms and legs call for rest and refreshment ; do not make a false move by asking a lot of questions, or trying to lead the conversation, lest all should close up like oysters, but make discreet offerings to Bacchus, and to Pluto, or whoever may be the god of bacca, and keep your ears wide oh.

Captain Joe Jentleman, the landlord, was a retired coasting skipper, of the old school, with a voice like a foghorn, and a hard fist, always at hand to pass out the foaming pots through the little bar window, or to settle an argument that promised to finish in a row ; Mrs. Jentleman was a pattern housewife, and kept the place, and the mugs, and jugs, as clean as the next one, and when her work was done she would come and stand behind the settle, just able to peep over the top, where she would listen to the conversation, and sometimes chip in with a shrewd remark.

An Ancient, known as Gaffer, held the place of honour nearest the fire, by right of seniority, which enabled him to get the best of many an argument by going back some years before his opponent was born. " Gaffer," said Captain Joe, " jest look ware you are a squotting that bacca juice, your beard is dreepin with it tew ; " " Ah,

Captain," says Gaffer, "I allus was wunnerful fond of a bit er bacca for the tooth, fifty yare agoo, an more, owd Dr. Mannell, him wot used to live over the water, Puzzleguts they used to call him, he come to see me once wen I was laid by, and he say to me, says he, Ephy Bor, says he, if yaou chow sa much terbacca yaou'll kill yarself, and owd Dr. Mannell he 'a bin dead years an years and hare am I well and hearty, and I chow a sight er bacca.

"I can see how it is Captain, owd fooks is in the way now, and as sune as yaou begin to git a little bit owd yure shuffed a oneside, and nobody don't want yer." "All right Gaffer," says the landlord, "don't get snaasty about nothin, here come Blazer Brown, and now we shall hear the news. Lor, his gills are some red, whereever ha'yew bin Blazer? yar face is as red as Martlesham Lion." "Bin," says Blazer, "why I'a bin to a meetin about this here water job, and we 'a had a proper barney; wot I say is we don't want no waterworkses. Pint o'old and mild please Master, and not so much o' that froth this time."

"I'm with you there," says the captain, wiping the bottom of the mug, and handing it over. "There's plenty enow water for the likes of us in our pumps, as good as any I ever got when I was at sea, and I 'a filled up in all sorts o' ports. Gord ha' give us plenty o' good water and now these new fook come, and want to shove waterworks and pipes into us, interfarin with Gord I call it, and no good'll come on it you'll see."

"Thass all right owd Captain," chimed in a younger fisherman, who answered to the nickname Toshes, on account of his prominent teeth, "thass all right for you and I, we 'a had to drink some funny stuff in our times, but we were browt up on it, now these here wisitor fooks they come down, and wen they fust drink our water out o' the well my Missis tell me that wholly scour 'em, and I did hare as how tew or three o' them there London doctor blokes writ to the papers about it and us wot let lodgins we don't want no nonsense like that."

"Is that right Tosh," ventured another customer, "wot I did hare say as how larst time yar well was cleaned out they found a dorg in it? if that wore so why then thass no wonder the fooks got the back-door trots a drinken on it, 'tis a miracle they wornt kilt."

"The water ain't so bad," put in a tall fair-haired descendant of the Danes, known to his cronies as the Eelpicker, "but wot I say is that want a drop o' suffin in it ter kill the miscrobes, if anyone is a goin to stand me a glass o' our water with a tot o' rum in it, I ain't a goin ter hang back. All the same I'd allus suner have a drop o' bare, thass one thing, the water may be bad, but there ain't no bad bare, some bares is better 'an other bares but there ain't no bad bare." "Jesso, Eelpicker," retorted Toshes, "but don't forget ' wen bare is

in wittles is out' as pore owd Ben Only used ter
say, and don't let that make a fule on ye, what
d'yew say Gaffer? "

"Well," said the Ancient, from his corner, " I
don't howd a lot with these foreners, but dessay
there might be suffin in it for them, the water suit
me right well, but fooks hain't all got the same
innards, there's one thing about it, whativer happen,
I spose we shall all live till we die." Did I iver
tell you together about owd Summers and the
musharune wine, well that was time they wore a
buildin some half and halfers on the beach, must
be sixty yare agoo, whativer more, and me, and three
or four other owdacious young warmin used to go
down and play the min up, steal the chips, and
titter ma tauter on the timber, and the likes o'
that; owd Bob Wincop was the hid man, I spect
you'v heerd o' Bob Wincop's broad hints, a way
he had o' talking, so he say to us, he say, ' Sling
yer hook yer young davils, and thass a broad hint,'
but as we dint take it he played artful and he say,
' arn't you together dry runnin about with nothin
to drink? ' ' Times we are,' we said. ' Well
then,' says he, ' if you goo and knock at Mr.
Summerses backus, and ax him right nicely
haps he'll gon you some o' his musharune
wine.

" So orf we goo, jest down the rood, ware owd
Summers used ter live, and knocked at the doer,
by and bye the owd man come and opened it, he
looked wunnerful owd at us, but howsiver I up

and towd him as Mr. Wincop should say if we axed him nicely haps he'd give us a glass o' his musharune wine. Lor, I'd hardly got the words out afore he come at us with a great stick, like a roary bull, ' Musharune wine you young warmin,' he say, ' I'll gi you musharune wine wen I catch yer,' and he runned us, blorin like the town bull, till he was poke-blown and we climbed up on to one o' the big botes, wot was hauled up there, ware we knew he coon't git, and then we called him all the funny owd things we could think on to torment him, till he went orf home a foamin at the mouth, and wen we looked there was owd Bob a laughin fit ter rupture hisself.

"By Gum; we used ter hev some fun them days, and boys worn't spylt wi' sa much larnin as they fare ta be now I don't howd wi sa much on it, we are properly pyzened a larnin now a days, look a' that gal Naomi, my granddarter, wot dew you think Mrs. Jantleman, Mam, they a bin a teachin o' har up a' that skule?

"All about them there owd kings an' queens, wot d' she want to know about them for? they 'a bin dead hundeds o' yares, let 'em lay I say, and let har keep at home and hope har mother."

"Thass right Gaffer," put in Mrs. Jentleman, from behind the settle, "the galls I get now don't know nothin any good to 'em, and I have to teach 'em everything what they ought to have larnt at home, and pay 'em while I'm a teachin 'em;

eddication is all werry well but that 'ont keep a house clean, nor yet cook a dinner."

"Never mind Mother," interposed her husband, "let the mawthers alone to-night for thass jest on closin time and so we'll wish you gentlemen all good-night."

II

NOT SO SILLY

LONG years ago, before the days of Mr. Bruce, and the Public House Closing Act, in a large village in Mid-Suffolk, dwelt a prosperous, and canny old farmer, whom I will christen Dan Ghoate, for the occasion, whose custom it was sometimes to sell a beast to the local butcher, to be killed and paid for according to the dead weight, after it had been dressed.

On one occasion he so disposed of a fat bull to his butcher friend, and in due course went down to see the carcase weighed ; to his surprise and vexation the weight was not nearly as much as he expected, and he expressed himself plainly about it ; the butcher, however, said there it was and he could see for himself there was no inside fat, and he would have to put up with it.

So after some haggling the matter was settled, the money paid, and Master Ghoate departed, still feeling unhappy about the late bull.

During dinner he was told the yardman wanted to see him, and stepping out the man said, " Th' owd bull is home Master." " Oh, is he though," said the farmer, " do you go and shut him up in the box, and I'll come and see about him." So dinner over with much content, Mr. Ghoate went out, and satisfied himself it was in truth his deceased bull come home again. He then had him fed, locked up the door, put the key in his pocket, and told his man that if any one came after the bull, he wasn't to know anything about him, except that he heard his master say that he was kilt, and paid for.

With the money in his pocket this simple Suffolk farmer set out in his gig, called on all his friends, and invited them to meet him at the Hare and Hounds for a spree ; the company having assembled they sat themselves down and ate, drank, and enjoyed themselves, day and night, and never left the premises, until the whole of the price of the bull was spent.

And so Farmer Dan, and his friends made merry at the expense of the dishonest butcher, who never had the face even to claim the bull, which reads rather like a tract.

The same simple soul always carried two purses, one well lined for use, and the other empty, which he would pull out, and display with well assumed regret if anyone wanted to borrow from him.

When I was a boy we had a tall, stalwart steward, a very useful and valued man, who lived on the premises, with his rather decrepit old father, quite past work. One day William came round and told

my mother it was his father's birthday, that he had
given him a new great coat, and that the old chap
would very much like her to see it. So round they
came, the father in a very useful blue cloth coat,
which seemed rather loose for him, and was
practically sweeping the ground. My mother
duly admired it, and the owner walked about,
and turned round as proud as a dog with
two tails.

Taking an opportunity she remarked, *sotto voce*,
to the son, " Don't you think it rather large for
him?" and with an almost audible wink this long-
headed son replied, " Well Maam, he 'ont want it
for long so I had it made to fit myself."

———

Two Suffolk labourers met on the road one day,
" Mornin John," says one. " Mornin t'yew
Garge," replied the friend, " what are you a dewin
on saanterin about this time o' day? " Oh, I'm
out o' work," says John, " lookin for a place, dew
you know of one? " " Why sartinly," replied
Garge, " my Master 'll gi you a place if you 'a got
a character, but thass no use your axin him if you
han't got no character ; Ha' you got one? "
" In coorse I have," Garge made answer, " but I
'a lorst it." " Whaat ? " says his friend, " lorst yer
character, well you must be a duzzy fule." " Ah
Bor," says John, " yow won't sah so if yow'd 'a
sin it."

———

Long ago it was related by Archdeacon Groome, in *Two Suffolk Friends*, that a balloon was carried over Suffolk, and coming low down at Monk Soham to ascertain their position, it passed over a labourer at work in a field. In response to frantic yells of " Where are we ? " there was borne upward the faint reply, " Yar up in a balune Bor," and the balloonists swept on, gnashing their teeth, no doubt, while Garge would chuckle to himself at having scored off some of " them forreners." I apologise for this chestnut, but have been asked to insert it as a typical Suffolk story from a book now very scarce and only accessible to a few.

Major-General Sir John Adye states in his *Soldiers and Others I have known*, that about 1880 " My battery had about thirty Militia Reserve posted to it, some from Scotland, some from Ireland, and some from the Eastern Counties ; no greater difference in type could be found in these islands than these men presented, and the unanimous opinion of the battery was that they preferred the stolid yokels from Norfolk and Suffolk who, whilst less quick at the uptake, were sober, steady, and well behaved."

In the days when the Blyth was navigable to Blythburgh bridge, and Sowl Trinity Fair was the great local event of the year, a ship lay at the bridge, with several Solemen in her crew, the Master refused them leave to go to the fair, so they said well then we may as well go to sea and persuaded the captain to drop down the river that tide; strange to say, between Blybro bridge and Southwold, that ship sprang a sudden leak, and made so much water that they had to tie up again at Blackshore quay, and the crew went to the fair after all.

There are of course hundreds of howlers from all parts, but here are a few Suffolk ones, which show that the youngsters in our National schools can hold their own with amusing, but shrewd replies :

What did Moses say when he struck the rock ?
Answer from a bright boy : " Howd yer mugs."

What did God make on the second day of the Creation ?
" Please Maam he made some furmetty " (an old Suffolk dish of wheat boiled in milk with sugar and spice).

In a lesson occurred a reference to a foal and its dam. The Mistress enquired of a boy what a dam was.

"Please Teacher," was his reply, "a dam mooter."

And a Master enquiring what an unclean spirit was, received the prompt reply that it was a dirty devil.

A small urchin, who had been severely lectured, and threatened with the wrath of heaven for stealing his neighbour's flowers, said to his chum one day, "It's very cloudy this morning, and I don't believe God could see me if I was to pluck a flower," and he took the risk.

After a lecture on wrecks and the use of the "Breeches Buoy", a Suffolk schoolboy wrote that a crew had been rescued by the "Butcher's Boy."

Many years ago there was a Southwolder, long departed this life, who was from time to time, a source of trouble to the authorities there, but all the same possessed a dry and caustic wit, which was a cause of frequent joy to his contemporaries ; on the occasion of a rather hectic Boro' Election, when a crowd was awaiting the verdict of the poll, our Suffolk droll mounted a cart and propounded this riddle to the assembled burgesses :

"What does the Corporation of Southwold resemble?" and no solution being given he announced, "The answer gentlemen is, hell in a mousetrap."

That reminds me of a still more ancient legend attached to Southwold market place, before the days of railways when every little townlet of that class was, more or less, a clan of mutually supporting denizens.

It is related of those ancients that now and again on a day of hopeless weather, when trade was at a standstill, and customers kept to their firesides, some leading, convivial tradesman would proceed to the Market place and fire a gun, whereupon all the other shopkeepers would put up their shutters, and assemble at the Old Swan to spend the rest of the day in worshipping the flowing bowl amid cheery surroundings.

I remember one of those quaint old birds who would drain his mug to the bottom, then, turning it upside down, let the froth drip on the floor, while he declaimed in rich and reverent tones, "Let us pray."

A worthy old soul went from Mid-Suffolk for a day by the sea at Yarmouth, but she did not go afloat, because as she said, "If anything happens to one of them there boats there's no back door

to get out of." She also enquired on her first sight
of the sea, " Dew that allus goo muddlin about
like that."

A couple of cottages down by some marshes in
East Suffolk, had one of those shallow dip wells
worked by a long pole, balanced on a crotch fixed
by the side of the well, the bucket was hooked
on the small end, which was then pulled down
until the water was reached, and the bucket filled,
then the weight of the large end of the pole would
bring the full bucket up without much effort ;   out
in the East these are known as " Shadoof Wells,"
and although this particular one has now disappeared there are a few still left in Suffolk in low
lying places.

It so happened that the ladies of these two
cottages, having quarrelled, were hardly on speaking
terms, and one of them came to complain to the
landlord about her neighbour, " For," said she,
" I'd planned to brew o' Monday, and time I was
gittin things ready, I could hear Mrs. Catt a routin
about in her place, and hullin water out at the back,
and what dew you think that owd article had bin
and done ? Why, when I went to the well with my
bucket to fill the copper, drat me if she han't bin and
drawed all the water out 'n the well, carried it in at
her front doer, and hulled it out at the back.

" In coorse, the water that would come slow
and thick arter that, and so I was done for that

morning, and there was that owd willain standin
at har doer a grinnin all over, and then, cos I up
and towd hat she was as holler as a Salvation
Army drum, she had the audacity to say I was a
walkin brewery, which I hain't bin near a public
for weeks, and then she patted har behind as
much as to say I could talk to that, and went in
and shet the doer.

"I and my owd man thowt haps you'd tell us if
we could give har a piece o' paper for that, cos she
dint ought to go orf that way."

Another, long deceased, Suffolk character was
distinguished for his craftiness over a deal during
the week, and his voluble and sanctimonious
prayers and sermons in the Meeting House on
Sundays ; but on one occasion he was badly had
by one of his " meetiner " friends, and was moved
to pray for him publicly the following Sunday :
" Oh Lord, look down upon brother Midders,
and chastise him for his evil ways. Come down
through the ruff Lord, and howd him over the
bottomless pit, howd him there Lord so he may
repent of his wickedness, don't drop him in dear
Lord but shug him well."

A notorious old poacher and receiver, happened
to drive by a Suffolk covey one day, just as the

owner, and his guests, had finished shooting it. The Guns, keepers, and beaters, were all assembled by the roadside counting the bag, the old rogue pulled up abreast of them for a moment, and called to the headkeeper, " John bor, you might let me ha' the rest o' them bahds as sune as con-wenient," he then whipped up his pony and departed at a handgallop, leaving the keeper speechless, but foaming with rage and mortifica-tion, and the rest of the party grinning.

A tenant on the same game infested estate, when called upon to make a return of the stock on his holding, took great pleasure in adding at the foot in bold writing, " And the devil and all of old hares."

In the old sailing days, when a man had been brought up a sailor, his language would savour of the sea to his last day, e.g., an old salt had been engaged as a beater, and at the end of a drive, when hardly a bird had been seen, he was asked if he had seen any, and where they went. " Oh yes," said he, " I see plenty o' bahds, some went to the west'ard, some to the east'ard, but most on em bore up into the norrard, and went orf afore the wind."

A parvenu sportsman to Suffolk, developed a habit of always coming short of cartridges, and borrowing from other Guns, so an old farmer planned to give him a lesson, and asked him one day by himself.

After shooting a couple of hours or so, the guest came short as usual, and went to his host to borrow, whereupon the latter said, " I spose then you've had all the shutin you expected to git, and so we'll go home," and home they went.

———

A Suffolk keeper, of the old school, remarked of a Gun, who had taken to shooting too late in life to shine at it, and was a source of quiet amusement to others, " Mr. Jones is no spootsman, but he make spoot for other people."

———

A similar old boy called out to his unseen brushers inside a wood, " How many on ye is there in there? " Voice from within, " What dew you say? " " How many on ye is there in there? " The voice, " There's tree on us." " Then haalf on ye come out hare."

———

Years ago an old girl told me this story of my grandfather and her father, both of whom died before I was born, and it gave her much pleasure in the telling, which was as follows :

" My father was a rough carpenter at Walberswick, and the first time he was sent for to do a job at Blybro Lodge he set off after breakfast to see what was wanted, and make a start ; on his way he met your grandfather on hossback. ' Hullo, Lusher,' he say, ' this won't do for me you know, six o'clock in the morning is my time.' ' All right Sir,' said my father, I won't forgit.' Soon after dinner he found he could not get any fudder without some more tools, so he thought it best to knock off, and come again the next day. On the way home, drot me, if he dint fall in with your grandfather again. ' What,' says he, ' you're never goin home ariddy ? ' ' Yes Sir,' said my father, ' I thought bein as I begun late I'd better make up for it by goin home early '. ' Huh,' said your grandfather, ' I allus heard you were a dam rum feller, and now I know it.' He was a wunnerful man for lookin arter his people your grandfather was."

We have been hearing a good deal about tithe lately, and I am reminded of a Southwold story of the days prior to the Tithe Commutation Act of 1836, when tithe had to be paid in kind.

A new Vicar came who was very keen on his rights, and amongst other things demanded a tithe of the fish caught. This as may be supposed, caused a considerable rumpus on the beach. He was defied for some time, until things got so threatening some of the men decided to give it, and one day a body of them marched to the Vicarage, and shot several bushel skeps of fish down in the hall, saying they had brought their tithe; but it was fish they had caught several weeks before, and had kept for the purpose.

I recollect some visitor, in the days when Dunwich Church was plainly visible from Blybro Lodge, stopping one of our people to ask the way there. He directed him the proper road, and said it was about four miles, whereupon the visitor enquired if there wasn't a nearer way straight across the marshes. "Yes," was the reply, but you marn't goo that way." "Oh never mind that," said the summer man, "you just shew me, and I'll take the risk."

"Well then," said Silly Suffolk, "dew you find out," and so left him.

III

GHOSTS AND GHOSTESSES

I THINK there can really be no doubt that many self-respecting Ghosts have retired from active service, this restless, hustling, changeable, age must have driven them off the road, like many other little old-fashioned people. Take Black Toby, the Blythburgh Ghost, about whom I wrote in my "Suffolk Coast Garland," what chance would he have, with his hearse, and four headless horses, on the Turnpike at midnight? He would almost certainly be run down, and destroyed by one of those huge meat vans, or some juggernaut of a six-wheeled lorry, tearing down from London by night; and even in houses, electric light, and bells, wireless, telephones, and other modern inventions must discompose a Family Ghost who naturally cannot be expected to move with the times.

Yet Mr. Beverly Nicols gave, us in his " Twenty-Five," I think, a genuine West Country mystery, which he, and other bright young people, failed signally to clear up. I saw the derelict house in question not long after, and was told by a friend near by that it was said there had been a murder in that house long ago, and that there was certainly something very uncanny about the place.

So it is possible that psychic people may still be able to see spectral apparitions, under favourable circumstances, especially those born at the chime hours, that is, at 4, 8, or 12, and we may still go on telling ghost stories.

Anyway superstitious folk are still about, and things that go bump in the night yet scare many nervous people, so quite naturally the company round the fire at the Half and Halfer got a thrill when Bumper Bird told them about the man found drowned in one of the creeks nearby the day before.

" Me and Stumpy were a goin down to the quay afore daylight to goo orf a trawlin, that was jest afore low water, and the wind was orf, what little there was and I stopped to light my pipe ; jest then I heerd some one a callin, ' Oooh,' like that, not wery loud, but plain enough, and I say to Stumpy, ' whew's that a hollerin ?' and he say ' Thass one o' Gord's forsaken ones that is, don't us take no nottis o' that, look where the wind lay, straight from Gord's yard, and thass one o' them what can't rest ; come on.'

" But just then I heerd it agin, and so did he, ' Oooh,' that say, and I tell ye that wholly made my flesh crawl, and owd Stumpy, he was properly scared too ; I says less goo and git a light, and see if we can find anyone.

" ' Bor,' he say, ' if you goo to look arter that you'll see suffin you 'ont like, I tell ye thass some-one what can't lay quiet, and that ain't for the

likes of us to interfare along o' that. Come on less
we be a goin dew we shall miss the tide.'

"So away we went, and niver heerd no more,
we trawled the whole flood, and then had to beat
back, so that was wery nigh half ebb when we got
in, and as we were a goin up home, Jacko come
acrost to us from the Crick, and say, ' We'a jest
found a man drownded in there,' and so we went,
and some folks were then a gettin on him out, he
was in the mud up to his waist, and we could see
where he had walked in at low water time, and got
stuck; missed the rood way somehow in the
dark; he was a stranger to us, and looked like a
trampin feller, and I say to Stumpy, I lay thass
whew we heered singin out this mornin.

"I spose someone towd the Pleece that, 'cos I
had to goo on the Hall to-day, and tell the Crowner
what we heerd, and he said no doubt that was the
man, and that we did ought to a gone, and got him
out, and that he must ha' bin drownded when the
tide rose; so they give it as accidental death by
drownin, but I don't think they know whew the
man is; if I'd a knowed what I know now we'd a
gone arter him, but thass a funny thing to know
what to dew of a night time on a job like
that."

"Ah," said an old retired pilot, "very likely
you'd a gone, and looked for hours, and never
dropped on to him, 'cos he must ha' bin under
water soon after the tide flowed. I well recollect
one time when I was in the cutter, I had the watch

alone one night, and stood at the tiller looking round, but there was nothing in sight except a steamboat, or two, miles away. When all of a sudden I heard some one sing out, ' Ship ahoy ', on our port quarter, and I looked but I couldn't see any craft anywhere, then I heard it again right plain, ' Ship ahoy,' and I shoved the tiller down and runned to the companion-way and hollared down, ' Here tumble up quick, here's some poor devil afloat,' and up they come and launched the boat as quick as possible ; they pulled all round and I kept torching for an hour or more, but we never see, nor heard anything, and I can't tell ye now whether that was a man, or someone from Fiddler's Green, you know, where the drowned sailors go."

Apropos of people not resting in their graves, Forby, in his East Anglian Vocabulary, tells of a tradition in a Suffolk coast village, that a man ordered he was to be buried with his head to the east, otherwise he wouldn't lie quiet in his grave. When he died this wish was neglected, or forgotten, and he was buried in the usual way.

Before long a rumour arose that he was walking, and several people stated definitely that they had seen him wandering round the churchyard ; this report presently made so much noise in the place that his people had the coffin dug up and reburied as he wished, after which the deceased was never seen again. Forby wrote this just over one hundred years back and stated the grave was then to be seen with the headstone at the east end, but gives no nearer clue to its identity. Fifty years after a writer in the Ipswich Journal *Notes and Queries* asked for information about this grave, but I could not trace any reply.

An animated discussion followed Bumper's narration and it was plain that the majority of the Half and Halfers were firm believers in ghosts. One man related that another of those restless ones was well known in Covehithe Churchyard, where she walks about dressed all in white, and those who had seen her asserted that she had no face. Another told of the shrieking woman of Southwold, said to be the widow of a fisherman who had been drowned, and who went crazy watching for him to come home, and jumped off the North Pier. When she is seen about the cliff it is a sure sign of a gale.

The Eelpicker was then emboldened to say he had seen " owd Dr. William's ghost " ; that he had been on the clift early one morning, and going round a corner he ran right up against him, whereupon Mrs. Jentleman, who was listening from behind the settle, put her nose over, and said, " Why didn't you pay the man for his pills Picker, then he wouldn't harnt you ? "

There was a shout of laughter at this sally, and a facetious customer enquired what he said to the Doctor. " Nothin," said Eelpicker, " I didn't think that was my place to speak fust, and he never said a word to me."

" Ah well," said Gaffer, "you may laugh, but us old ones know right well that the night the Clipper was lost, the grandmother of two of the crew see them right plain, walkin up the street ahid o' her; she wondered what they was home for so she followed them, but before she could catch them up they wanished. She towd iverybody about it and said suffin had happened and sure enough the word come in a day or two the boat was missin, and none of 'em was ever picked up, nor nobody dint niver know how she was lost."

There is a tradition that some wicked squire haunts the Wangford-Reydon road, near Reydon Hall, and a man driving past there once about midnight was nearly thrown out of his cart by his horse shying, and stopping dead. When he looked, there was a coach and four in the road, and of course the horses had no heads, still when the coachman whipped them up they trotted off and the man got home safely.

There used to be a high, thick, holly fence at this spot, since replaced by a brick wall, and there was something about it that horses did not like, to which I can testify having often had difficulty in getting my hunters past. About 1900, when Jack Reeve, groom from the Swan at Southwold, was bringing a new hunter from Norwich, for the late Mr. Adnams, the horse shied there, Reeve was thrown off, and killed on the spot, a tragedy which of course gave new life to an old legend.

And now let me wind up this chapter by relating what I believe to be absolutely true, and perhaps shed a little light on those churchyard ghosts ; a very good chum of my youth, who was one of the finest, and boldest of our Suffolk country folk, of the fairhaired, blue-eyed, Northman type, a farmworker who had followed the water as a youngster, and was afraid of nothing.

He told me that on one occasion the sexton was laid up, and he agreed to dig a grave for him one Saturday afternoon, and got it about half dug when a very heavy thunderstorm came on, and he had to leave it.

Late that evening the sky cleared, and the moon came out bright, and my friend thought he might as well go and finish the grave so as not to lose any time over it ; so away he went, and when he got there he found the flood water had drained that way, and the grave was half full of water, so he had to go back home and get a bucket to bail it out, and by that time it was well past closing time, and no one about. He began to bail the water out, and presently heard someone coming up the street, whistling away as he approached the churchyard, to keep up his spirits ; my friend had on his usual white slop, and was stooping down to fill the bucket, and then rising to empty the water out.

He saw the man stop and look at him, whereupon out of " daviltry," as he said, he stood straight up, and raised his arms up above his head. " Lor,"

said he, "that faller set orf a runnin like a scalt
cat, and I could hare him all the way till he got
home, and banged his door arter him, and then I
went to work and finished that grave by midnight,
and I lay that chap thowt he'd sin a ghoost to his
dyin day."

IV

OH PILOT 'TWAS A FEARFUL NIGHT

LOOKING for a berth in the evening train one day,
ah! more than twenty years back, I heard a cheery
hail. " Hi, Mister, come in here," and looking
round I saw the face of an old North Channel
pilot friend of mine, a face that told of hard, cold
times at sea, and stuffy inn parlours ashore with
unstinted tobacco and grog. I stepped in and
soon perceived by the interested, tittering, company,
and by other unmistakable signs, that my friend
was in the happy garrulous state known on the
coast as " Cherry-Merry, not drunk you know,
but had a glass," and had been entertaining his
fellow travellers with some samples of Suffolk
humour. I enquired for the news and was informed
he had been up with a ship, and at the Saracen's
Head had fallen in with some old shipmates, and
had a " bewtiful time, BEWTIFUL, some of the
best rum along of the London River."

A gentleman in the N.W. corner thereupon
expressed the opinion that rum was " wunnerful
good for a cowd, but not much water with it."

" Talking of rum," said the Pilot, " begging
your pardon, Mister, but that was a drop of good

40

rum I had aboard of your little craft at Harwich that time." I expressed my ignorance of the incident and gently led my Trinity House friend to tell of this remarkable rum.

" Why," said he, " you must recollect being up at Harwich that time when owd Duke was with you, him what used to go along with us in the cutters, thass years ago now, but I'll never forgit it if I live to be a thousand. I'd been up with a ship and got back to Harwich in the evening, just like it might be to-night. I looked in at the Alma to leave my bag and hew should I see settin there but Duke. ' Cheeroh ! Duke bor,' says I, ' what the davil are you dewing here all this way from home ? ' ' Yachtin',' says he, ' layin' in the Pound, we beat up under the Ness afore breakfast this morning ; but that come a fresh wind at Nothe East on the flood and so we bore up, and the Guv'nor, he's gone home by train. I'm to take her home when we get a shift, so I'm on my own, and I hope this wind will last a week.'

" And so you know we spent the evening together and wherever we went there was friends, Harwich was chock full of them. My flesh that was a wet night, and, when Bruce's time come and we was pushed out, we went down to the steps to look for the cutter's boat, and o' course she was gone, tired o' waitin I spose.

" ' There you are Duke,' says I, ' wos to be done now ? Everywhere closed up and we've got the key of the street.' ' Never mind,' says he, ' you come and sleep along o' me aboard o' the yacht, an in the morning I'll give you a shove off to the cutter. Come on! The pram lay alongside of the old Zion.'

" So we gets aboard of the smack and Duke he drops down into the little bote alright, but I aren't used to them tittley little concarns and so I lights onlucky, and over we goes into the ditch, both on us. Beggin your pardon Mister—it worn't just a matter of goin overboard, she threw me yards, yards she did, I never see such a tittley little affair. So there we were, both on us, in the Pound, in the dead o' night and not a soul near. ' O dear! o dear,' says Duke, splouncin about, ' whatever shall we do. Sing out John,' says he, ' sing out, dew we shall be drowned.' ' Hold your tongue, yer long davil,' says I, ' and don't make all that tarnition row, d'you want to be in the East Anglian in the mornin?' says I, and I got him by the back of the neck and swum off to the yacht, only a matter of a few yards, and catchin howd of the mizzen sheet I seized his wrist up to the riggin and let him hang while I gets aboard, then I tied a rope round his waist, hooked on the main halliards and soon had him aboard, nose and knees together like a drownded dorg.

" Well, after we had recovered the little bote, and stowed things up a bit, down we goes and pullin off our wet close gets under the blankets, but I han't been there long when I begins to dudder. ' Duke,' says I, ' I think I've took a chill.'

' Howd on,' says he, ' I believe I know where the owner keeps his rum.' Beg your pardon Mister, but that was a drop o' good rum, I don't know where you got it, but that was a rare drop, and that saved our lives that night time we'd finished it, what there was of it."

The narration of this yarn, with endless interjections and repetitions, interrupted by roars of laughter from the audience, delighted by the drollery of the delivery as much as by the matter, carried us well on the journey, and, after begging pardon for the *n*th time, the Pilot dropped into somewhat stertorous slumber, while I let my mind wander back to that Harwich trip of long ago. I recollected that getting under way at three o'clock on a pitchy dark morning after the Regatta, well reefed down to a strong N.E. wind, then turning to windward for five hours in a nasty sea, the bitter easterly dawn, and the conference when the tide turned, and we could not hold our own—old Duke's expert advice to turn back, and his remark when I seemed reluctant to give in—" Well we can go in close under Orford Beach and bring up till high water, but you won't like it," I recalled roaring back to Harwich, before the wind and tide, the " tittley little consarn " tearing along behind, and mooring again in the Pound by nine o'clock, five hours out and one back and no forrarder, but that way men were made in the days of sail.

It also came back to me that when Duke and yacht eventually returned and I suggested that a tot of rum would do him good after a long day, that ancient mariner blandly replied, " She upset the bottle comin round the Ness," then, seeing a somewhat incredulous smile on my face, he added in an injured tone, " well thass the truth and if you don't believe me you can smell the towel what was in the same locker," after which tender of indisputable evidence there was no more to be said, but now I could see daylight and the real truth was worth a whole bottle at least ; good old Dukey, peace to his ashes, he was a real sailor man and I absorbed much sea lore from him.

When we were far away from home and conversation flagged, Duke would come out with one of his stock witticisms, " There's hundeds don't know where we are," then after a considerable pause during which he would look all round the horizon, he would finish it by declaiming " And there's thousands don't care."

Once during a regatta, at which we were competing, Duke ran out of " chewing bacca," and as he was so excited that he must have something, I gave him a cigarette which he unrolled, and crammed into his mouth, but it was like chaff for that purpose, and as he chewed, and chewed, the fragments dribbled out of both corners of his mouth till he was a quaint sight.

A grinding of brakes and groaning of buffers and the train pulls up at Manningtree, the Pilot sleepily gathers himself together, stumbles out with his

painted canvas bag, and takes a few steps, then
swings round and returns to put his rubicund,
hearty, old face in at the window, " Beggin your
pardon Mister, but that was a drop of good rum.
Goodnight all."

V

ROUGH NOTES

THE migration of birds has been observed in East Anglia for some centuries. Sir Thos. Browne, of Norwich, 1605-1682, was one of the earliest to write about it, and he laid down that there were two great annual invasions, spring and autumn. He said "Many are discoverable both in winter and summer which are of a migrant nature and exchange their seats according to the season, those which come in the spring coming for the most part from the southward; those which come in the autumn or winter from the northwards, so that they are observed to come in great flocks with a N.E. wind and to depart with a S.W., nor to come only in flocks of one kind but teals, woodcocks, felfars, thrushes and small birds to come and light together, for the most part some hawkes and birds of pray attending them."

Dan. Defoe made his observations on the departure of the swallows in 1724-5 from his lodgings by Southwold Churchyard, "I observed in the evening an unusual multitude of swallows sitting on the leads of the Church. This led me to enquire and I was answered that this was the season when the swallows, their food failing here, begin to leave us and return to the country, wherever it be, from whence they came and the wind contrary they might be said to be windbound. This was the more evident to me, when in the morning I found the wind had come about to the N.W. in the night and there was not one swallow to be seen."

At one time it was thought that many swallows and martins hibernated under water, and our dear old friend, Gilbert White, was persuaded they lay torpid in holes and caverns and came out on warm sunny days.

At present one of the great assembly places in Southwold is over Debney's shop the other side of South Green, and they generally go off in batches, no doubt others keep arriving from inland and the late hatched birds probably go last. The latest record I have is of a house martin seen November 19, 1923.

For many years records of the annual migrations have been kept in many countries, and one of the most remarkable is a series kept by four generations of the Marshams of Norfolk from 1736 to 1810, and from 1836 to 1874, dealt with in Vol. 2 of the Norfolk and Norwich Natural History Society. The phrase a " Bird of Passage " has become a stock saying in England and I suppose derives from the migratory habit.

Mr. A. H. Patterson gives a migration chart in his " Nature in Eastern Norfolk," and makes all the routes centre on Yarmouth, but we are just as much in the track here; the streams appear to be that the small shore and land birds come along shore, often almost in the breakers quite low, again as I lie in bed on autumn mornings I see them going south over the Green in bunches, by the flight many of these are finches and buntings, and as this goes on for days, by day and night, the numbers passing must be very great.

The oversea stream comes in autumn from the east to S.E., the rooks generally turn up within three days one way or the other, of the twenty-first of October, and seem to cross in the night. Woodcock come with the first October easterly gale; they sometimes strike the wires and chimney pots and some are picked up about the town most seasons, others pitch down on the cliffs or in private gardens but only stay a very short time. then pass on inland.

All night long in the season, if your window is open and your hearing good, the migrating call of the golden plover, and others of that tribe, can be heard, and on dark windy nights birds of all kinds may be seen twizzling round in the light-house beams quite bewildered. You get up one morning and find the trees alive with busy little goldcrests, which come right across the North Sea in flocks while the home fishing is on, and so are called " Herring Spinks " by the fishermen, as soon as they have had a rest and a bit of grub they move on inland like the woodcock.

This main oversea route of the autumn flight appears to be direct to North Suffolk, crossing the Island of Heligoland where Herr Gatke kept most painstaking records for some thirty years or more.

As a rule birds, and fish, know when a gale is coming on and make a move before it breaks. Cod will suddenly bite like mad, and herring and sprats will swim in determined fashion, and mesh themselves in thousands, when a few hours before there was nothing doing, almost for sure wind will follow and our men say " Ah them cod bit against that breeze," or " that breeze behind 'em made them herrin swim " and lucky the man who gets his lines, or his nets, before the gale arrives. The herring of course are migrating just the same as the birds, that is why they are classified by the scientists as pelargic, from the Latin meaning an overflowing stream, a flood.

Now and again, however, the birds are deceived and a S.E. wind suddenly flies round to N.W. and blows double strength, then the little travellers are caught half seas across and are drowned in multitudes. Some may doubt this theory of weather warning instinct because sometimes the birds and the gale arrive here together, but that is merely because they have been overtaken on the road.

I have seen the high water mark from here to the harbour, after one of those sudden northerly gales, almost black with rook's wings still fastened to the bare sternum, but all flesh and other feathers gone, cleaned up by the gulls and crows. Wood-

cocks and other of the larger migrants' wings will
also be found in small numbers, but no little birds
which are probably too fragile and get smashed up,
nor does one often see the relics of wild fowl on
those occasions. I imagine they are too strong on
the wing; anyone who has much experience of
fowl flighting in at night against a strong N.wester
knows they are no weaklings. Almost the only
thing that muddles wild fowl is snow, and that in
the ordinary way does not come until later.

It must be instinct, with the object of self-
preservation, which compels migration. Long
distances are covered by night when sight cannot
possibly help, and every year at least half the
travellers must be young birds who have never
made the journey before. It was stated by Tem-
minck that the young and the old travel apart,
and perhaps by different routes, so that they do
not depend upon guides; one of the most marvellous features being that the same birds return
year after year to their old nesting places, and young
birds find their way back to the district where they
were reared.

Migration is still something of a mystery to
us and must be the great adventure in life to the
birds themselves ; the casualties must be enormous,
but without it whole tribes of our feathered friends
would become extinct in very few years.

The International Conference on the Protection
of Migratory Wild Fowl held in London in October,
1927, and of which Lord Ullswater was chairman,

was a welcome indication that most European countries are alive to the growing need for protection if birds are to survive under the trying conditions of modern civilization.

The attractive feature about the spring immigation is that you appreciate the spirit of the medieval song,

" Sumer is icumen in, Loud sing cucko "

and feel that summer and its joys are ahead of you, otherwise I must say I find the autumn migration of greater interest to watch ; the birds can be seen in crowds during the shorter days, and do not appear by magic in ones and twos as they seem to do in the spring. The whole process is more of a struggle against nature, and the elements, by very fragile little people.

A Few Jottings from my Notebook

There is a tradition that if a swift alights on flat ground he cannot rise again, and I believe the heraldic martlet has neither feet nor legs, but early one morning in 1920, when I had a cottage on East Cliff, Southwold, I was awoke by something dashing in at the window, and falling on the floor. I saw it was a swift, and I watched it some minutes scrambling around on the bare boards. It certainly made very bad weather of it, but by and by it rose unaided from the floor and sailed out of the window again.

1923. October 19.—Dr. Hart Smith, of Acton Villa opposite, came across and told me that at twelve-thirty the previous night, during an easterly gale, he heard constant tapping at his bedroom window, and got up and opened it when in flew a bird and perched on the wardrobe. It was still there in the morning and he observed it carefully but when fully daylight it flew out of the window again and departed. He definitely identified it by Coward's "Birds" as a nutcracker, and we drew up a note and sent it to the *Field* for record.

Only about fifty nutcrackers have been recorded in Great Britain, where it is a rare autumn and winter visitor. Coward says the majority of the reports come from the southern and eastern counties and Babington records one taken at Holton in June 1824, and another at Southwold, prior to 1846, but date unknown.

1923.—During the last fortnight in October a snow-white house martin was regularly seen hawking on South Green, and was very interesting to watch as all his evolutions could be followed, and the same year I saw a sooty tern pass over the harbour quite close.

1924. February and March.—A seal established itself in the river. The Ferryman states that it climbs out on to the prow of the pontoon at night, and sleeps there, going off on his arrival in the early morning.

1925. April 19.—The rooks have returned to the trees in Southwold House garden ; up to about fifteen years ago there was a strong rookery there, but a new owner had most of the brick work whitewashed, whereupon the rooks deserted the place and never built there again until this year, by which time the whitewash had mostly gone ; the rooks continued to nest there until I left Southwold in 1931.

1925. May 10.—Visited the heronry by Blythburgh flats ; some young herons sitting out, about thirty nests this year. I had a splendid view of a spoonbill flying round with the herons over the island, he circled round two or three times, banking like an aeroplane with almost motionless wings and disappeared over the Bulcamp marshes. Cotton, the keeper, said it had been there a day or two and stated that he had counted sixty herons at one time ; I saw many pairs of shell fowl, which have increased largely about here since I was a boy.

August.—Saw a wheatear at the harbour, they are regular callers at that spot every summer.

1926. March.—The fishermen complain that there is a large seal in the bay which follows them and takes the herring out of their nets ; they say he sleeps on Dunwich Beach.

September 4.—Saw a cuckoo in our little back garden.

1927. May 17.—A redstart in ditto, and next month I saw a natterjack toad under the Gunhill, they seem to be getting scarcer of late years.

October 7.—Picked up a nightjar in the front garden, with one eye injured, probably by the wires; it soon died, another victim of progress.

October 16.—Rooks coming over by the harbour, and next morning I saw firecrests, great tits and blue tits all in the back garden together, and a very late swift hawking overhead.

1928. April 6.—Visited the heronry, twenty-three occupied nests, as far as I could tell; counted ten pairs of shell fowl on the flats. Cotton says there are still a number of woodcock in the woods.

May 7.—The Missis and I sailed up the river in the dinghy and through the breach in the Bulcamp wall just below Blythburgh Bridge; observed four turnstones, a dotterel, a cormorant or shag, a couple of pochards and many mallard and teal on the flooded area, which we sailed all over. Going down the river we got close to a party of godwits asleep in the sun, one still in grey winter plumage. I think this bit of flooded marsh, which dries out at half tide, brings a number of unusual water birds.

October 5.—Three snow buntings just arrived at the harbour, they generally drop in there every autumn.

1929. October 10.—The last two mornings, lying in bed, I have seen flight after flight of small birds going south; when I looked out at 7 a.m. there were flocks of martins wheeling round the Green, at seven-thirty they were all gone.

October 31.—Rooks coming over in flocks,

strong N.E. wind, small birds have been going south for weeks.

December.—Constant south and south west gales with torrents of rain. A hefty winter.

1930. January 28.—R.100 passed over at 9.30 a.m., quite low just clear of the land, and going S.W. Directly afterwards I noted a brambling on the road in front of the house. The bones of a mammoth are coming out of the cliff foot near Easton Broad ; my wife brought home part of a thigh bone, as much as two people could carry, and a molar and other oddments have been recovered.

May 13.—We observed a corn bunting in Easton Lane.

July 21 and 22.—N.W. gale, the whole Green swarming with swifts taking shelter, in the evening we saw hundreds hanging in bunches, like bees, from the louvres of the R.C. Church, later we heard from our daughter, at Aldeburgh, that Alde House was full of swifts sheltering. A most uncommon occurrence.

September 23.—A honey buzzard reported at Reydon, so I saw Mr. A. Clarke, of Reydon Grove, who told me he had put it up in a green lane at the back of his house, where it had dug out a wasp's nest, and was feeding on the grubs. He identified it by my Coward's plate.

September 28-29. Half a gale easterly all night, in the morning our trees were full of goldcrests, who remained about twenty-four hours, one was picked up dead and I weighed it on apothecary's scales and found it scaled sixty-eight grains, or just over one seventh of an ounce apothecary. So you could send fourteen of them by post for $1\frac{1}{2}$d. I had been shrimping in the morning and for curiosity put the largest brown shrimp I could find in the scales, and it weighed just about the same as the goldcrest, which I sent to a meeting of the Suffolk naturalists with this note.

1931.—Southwold Vicarage having been sold and turned into shops most of the elms in the garden were torn down and the rooks deserted that spot entirely after untold years of occupation. A few pairs went to Southwold House, but most of them left the town altogether, an ominous sign.

May.—A pair of penny wagtails built a nest under the deck planking at the outer end of the North Harbour Pier ; they laid five eggs and then deserted.

A pair of robins, for the second time in my life, built inside the old Lectern in Blythburgh Church ; they laid several eggs when unfortunately one bird was killed in a mouse trap in the church. I recollect a pair of robins bringing up a family behind one of the spandrils in the south aisle of that church ; they went in and out through a broken pane.

One autumn, date not noted, a merlin perched on our balcony rails one morning. Our sparrows were very upset, and when I opened the door one of them flew in and went upstairs as if the devil

was after him. The merlin moved to the window
sill and I watched him at a few feet distance ; he
was evidently very done after crossing, but, being
disturbed, he flew away down the Green, and was
shortly after " muddled to dead " by some boys.
I saw the deceased, a very handsome little fellow.

VI

PHILIP STAFFE—SHIP'S CARPENTER

AN HUMBLE HERO FROM IPSWICH

" History is the memory of time, the life of the
dead and the happiness of the living."
—CAPT. JOHN SMITH.

AFTER the Spanish bogie had been finally laid
by the defeat of Philip's great Armada, in 1588,
our hardy, enterprising seamen turned their attention again to exploration and discovery, in order
both to employ their restless spirits, and to seek
outlets for the growing trade of England and
work for her shipping. During the following
thirty years or so, very many voyages were made
in the little clumsy ships of the period, particularly
with the object of finding a shorter passage to
Cathay and the East, by the N.W. or N.E. routes,
either of which entailed great hardships in navi-
gating the Arctic Seas in order to get North of
the known coasts of Europe and America.

Among the great English merchant navigators
of the period, apart from the fighting Admirals,
who went on more or less buccaneering expedi-
tions, were John Davis, William Baffin, Martin

Frobisher, George Weymouth, North-West Foxe, and Henry Hudson—American writers speak of " Hendrick " Hudson, suggesting that Hudson River was first navigated by a Dutchman, because the *Half Moon* and her owners, as well as half the crew, were Hollanders ; but the matter has been definitely settled by the discovery of the contract, dated January 8, 1609, and made between " Mr. Henry Hudson, Englishman," and the East India Company of Amsterdam, who financed Hudson for that third voyage. Quite naturally, these enterprises originated at the great commercial ports, chiefly London and Bristol, which would, of course, benefit most by the opening up of new trade routes. Hudson's reports about the whales seen during his early voyages opened the Spitzbergen fishery to our whalers, and his discovery and exploration of the vast bay which bears his name, led directly to the establishment of the historic Hudson Bay Company.

Our Ipswich ship's carpenter, however, had no part in Hudson's third voyage, when the Hudson River was explored, but he formed one of the crew of the *Hopewell*, of eighty tons, about the size of our Ipswich coasting barges, in which Hudson made his second voyage. These voyages of Hudson were first collected and set down by the Rev. Sam Purchas, but it is owing to the researches of Mr. Powys, who wrote the Henry Hudson volume of the Golden Hind series, that we know more about the ships and their crews than is afforded us by

" Purchas His Pilgrimes." Powys says of Philip Staffe that he was an honest man from Ipswich, in East Anglia.

They sailed from London on April 22, 1608, and coasted along and about Novaya Zemlya, but were unable to discover anything like a North-East Passage, and, being much " impestered " by ice Hudson at last turned his back on the North Pole and arrived at Gravesend on August 26, 1608, having achieved very little beyond sighting a mermaid, who came close alongside and looked earnestly at the men. The captain noted in his log, " From the navill upward her backe and breasts were like a woman's—her body as big as one of us—and long hair hanging downe behinde, of colour blacke—her tayle speckled like a macrell."

Apparently our Ipswich man played his part honestly and well, for we find him shipping again as carpenter with Hudson for the fourth and last voyage, which was made in the *Discoverie*, a ship of only fifty-five tons, but having twenty-one of crew as against twelve in the *Hopewell*. She had been employed before on a similar quest by Capt. Weymouth, whose journals had also come into Hudson's hands.

Amongst the crew was Henry Green, a protégé of Hudson's, who, as so often happens in this base world, far from showing gratitude to, or supporting his benefactor, turned out to be the arch-villain of the piece, and the prime cause of the tragedies which came upon them. They sailed from the Pool

of London on the 17th April, 1610, and put into
Harwich on the 28th, where Green gave a foretaste
of his turbulent character by getting into a squabble,
but I feel sure the honest carpenter would embrace
the opportunity, and, taking one of the Passage
Boats, which then ran daily up the Orwell, pay a
visit to his native town to bid farewell to his
family and all Suffolk friends, and, perhaps, to have
a last word with Master Thomas Fuller, of Ipswich,
who went round the world with Cavendish, if
living.

The *Discoverie* sailed from Harwich on May Day,
and in due course, made Iceland ; there they fell
in with fog and contrary winds, and had to anchor
on the West side, where, going ashore, they found
a natural hot bath. One of the crew named Abacuk
Pricket also kept a journal, and he relates of this
spring that it was " So hot that it would scald a
Fowle and all our Englishmen bathed themselves."
Why the rest of the crew did not indulge he does
not say, but the name " Lousie Bay," which they
gave this anchorage, gives one furiously to
think.

From thence, Hudson stood across towards
Greenland, but found much ice, fog and snow,
so bad that the crew lost heart and began to jib.
Hudson asked them straight if they would go on
or go home, and one answered that if he had a
hundred pounds he would give four score and ten
to be at home, " sitting in my Dolphin Chamber,
at the round table, by a sea-cole fire," but then

upspoke our Suffolk Carpenter and made answer, "that if he had an hundred hee would not give ten upon any such condition, but would thinke it to be as good money as ever hee had any, and to bring it as well home, by the leave of God." And thus, "after many words to no purpose," the carpenter's staunchness carried the day and all hands turned to again. They then entered Hudson's Straits, and looking into Ungava Bay, coasted along until rounding a Cape, which he named after Sir John Wolstenholme, Hudson steered almost due South, and must have thought he had at last found the N.W. passage and was heading straight for the Pacific Ocean.

It was, however, only the entrance to the huge bay which now bears his name; and, sailing along the eastern shore, they were eventually caught by the winter quite at the bottom of the inlet called James Bay. There the carpenter and Pricket went ashore, and, having selected a site, Philip set to work, after vainly objecting that it was not a ship's carpenter's job, and put up a hut of sorts, and I quite think proved one of Hudson's best supporters through the trials and hardships of an Arctic winter. It is said that Fort Charles, the Hudson Bay Company's first fort, was built on the site chosen by Staffe for those winter quarters.

In the spring of 1611, when the ice began to melt, they refitted *Discoverie*, and eventually got her to sea, but sorely short of grub, which made the people discontented and suspicious that the master was concealing food from them. Consequently Green and two others named Juet and Wilson busied themselves hatching a plot to turn Hudson and the sick men adrift in the boat, in order that what food there was might go further amongst the reduced crew, and eventually, while still in the Bay, they put their plot into execution by fastening King, the boatswain, down in the hold, and then seizing and binding Hudson. They then put him, with his boy, Jack, and the sick men into the boat, and, having secured King, put him in also. The carpenter then appears to have come upon the scene, and, having no doubt, told them what he thought about it in downright good old Suffolk, asked them if they would be hanged when they came home. Now Pricket says the men disliked the carpenter, " because the master loved him, and made him mate in lieu of Billet, whereat they did grudge, for he could neither write nor read." This disability did not, however, prevent the carpenter from knowing his duty and carrying it out, notwithstanding that he might have remained in the ship, and perhaps have saved himself and all the rest, being the most capable and reliable man of the lot, even if he was illiterate. But, having made up his mind to stand for the right, and probably in the hope of being able to save his master and the other victims, the carpenter spoke out (according to Pricket), and " as for himself, hee said, hee would not stay in the ship unless they would force him ; and they bad him goe then, for they would not stay him. I will (said hee) so I may have my chest with mee, and all that is in it, they said he should, and presently they put it into the shallop. Then hee came downe to mee to take his leave of mee, who perswaded him to stay, which if he did, he might so worke that all should be well; hee said hee did not thinke but they would be glad to take them in againe. For he was so perswaded by the Master, that there was not one in all the ship, that could tell them how to carry her home; but (saith he) if we must part (which wee will not willingly doe, for they would follow the ship) hee prayed me, if wee came to the Capes before them, that I would leave some token that we had beene there, neere to the place where the Fowles bred, and hee would doe the like for us : and so (with tears) we parted. . . . The Carpenter got out of them a Peece and Powder and Shot and some Pikes, an Iron Pot, with some meale and other things . . . they cut her headfast from the sterne of our Ship then out with their Topsayles."

And so they parted, eleven hands remaining on board, while the " shallop " contained Henry Hudson, his son Jack, aged eighteen, who had been with his father on all these voyages, Philip Staffe and six others, of whom nothing more was ever heard, nor seen, except that twenty years after, Captain James, who wintered on Charlton Island, Hudson Bay, discovered there a row of stout stakes which had been sharpened by an European axe and which it is supposed were wrought by Staffe's hands, suggesting that the victims had reached land ; but no other trace was found. The mutineers sailed out of the Bay, and, on rounding the Cape, they saw a tribe of Esquimaux, who eventually fell suddenly upon a landing party and killed Green, W. Wilson, and two others, the rest getting away in the ship.

Old Purchas observes upon this " Wicked and wretched end of wretched, wicked men, and Miserie pursueth the rest," as was indeed the case, for the *Discoverie*, after drifting about for a month, was blown to the West Coast of Ireland. Juet died on the way, and the others were starved and almost demented. From thence they got a pilot, who took them to Plymouth, and the survivors were examined by Trinity House, who reported that they deserved to be hanged.

It was seven years after, however (1618), when Abacuk Pricket, Edwd. Wilson, Bennet Mathues and Francis Clemens appeared in the dock at Southwark, with sundry Pirates, and were charged with the murder of Henry Hudson and eight of the Company. They all pleaded Not Guilty, and threw themselves on the Country, which was another way of demanding to be tried by a Jury. The Jury found them not guilty (for want of evidence, probably), and they were discharged, but the pirates were duly hanged.

And so ended this tragedy of the sea, and none knoweth where the bones of the victims lie, but no man ever had greater or more enduring monuments, than Henry Hudson, of Hudson's Bay, in the Frozen North, and Hudson River, in the U.S.A., and with his name must ever be associated that of Philip Staffe, the Suffolk ship's carpenter, who shared his master's adventures and volunteered to accompany him in adversity—even unto death.

There was a William Staffe living at Chelmondiston in 1640, and it is likely that Philip was of that family, and worked in Ipswich shipyards before going to sea.

As I opened this brief story of a Suffolk worthy by quoting from a distinguished pioneer friend of Hudson, Capt. John Smith, of Virginia and New England I will close with another of his aphorisms " Seeing honour is our lives' ambition ; and our ambition after death to have an honourable memorie of our life, and seeing by noe meanes wee would bee abated of the dignities and glories of our Predecessors ; let us imitate their vertues to bee worthily their Successors."

After this came out in the *East Anglian Daily Times* a lady wrote to tell me that her brother was in the Hudson Bay country and that they were just about to erect a Memorial to Philip Staffe.

VII

CHAITS

" Broken victuals, the remains of turnips, or other food left by sheep."—(Moor's *Suffolk Words*).

This old Suffolk word seems to suit a chapter devoted to odds and ends.

It is told of Constable, the Suffolk artist, that, being dissatisfied with the quality of the milk supplied to him, he interviewed the milk man, and asked if he would oblige by delivering the milk, and water, in separate cans.

I do hope my readers will not find too much milk and water here, but had we not in Suffolk in the seventeenth century a gentleman named " Drinckmilke " and yet another called " Drinck-water."

I have an old prayer book which belonged to my great-grandfather, James Barber of Hopton, Suffolk, Lord of the Manor of Bacons, Gorleston ; it contains the Prayers for the 5th November Gunpowder Treason, The Form of Prayer with Fasting, for the 30th January, King Charles the Martyr, and Thanksgiving for the 29th May, 1660, Restoration Day, also Tate and Brady's metrical version of the Psalms ; but what interests me more is a scrap of paper I found shut up in it giving several prescriptions for the treatment of jaundice, in a script perhaps as old as Gunpowder Treason, and which seem worth putting on record.

"for ye ganders"

"Roast a Lemon and 1 Dram of tarminick ½ a Dram of saffrine squase ye Lemon upon these and put them in a pint of mounting wine and warm it".

————

"Take a handfull of ye inard bark of barbary sixty oweld sowes and a rusty hors shooe and Red hot and 3 quarts of oweld bear and put it into a bottle and drink it".

————

"Take a point of mountain wine and a panar of flower of brimstone—A panar of tarmarick and a panar of safan and put them into ye wine and drink it off a pot full at a time".

————

"Tarminick" I take it is tamarisk, "Oweld sowes" are our wood-lice, which were to be drowned in old beer with a red hot horse shoe; "Panar" is probably a pennorth, and the concoctions remind me of Lord Derby's famous verdict on the Antigout Claret, that he much preferred the gout.

The people who relied upon these remedies were of the same type as the labourer who went to, what he called, " the Chemister " and demanded a " pennorth o' pills to hull a woman into a sweat."

An old friend of mine, who used nux vomica in his poisoning operations, used to ask the " chemister " for " Ox Womit," and would get what he wanted ; the same old character never transplanted his seedlings, but always " strange-planted " them, which really seemed to suit the operation well.

———

A horseman had an awkward, troublesome, old horse in his team and one morning when he went to bait him there laid the old chap dead in the stall. " Drot ye," said Tom to the departed, " you ha' sarved me many a darty trick in yar time, but you niver sarved me that one afore."

Another who was watching some pigs fighting for the swill he had just given them, remarked, " Ah Bors you worn't called hogs for nothin."

———

I referred at page 31 of my " Suffolk Coast Garland " to the Huntingfield Volunteers doing duty at Southwold in 1805, and have since come upon " A Volunteer Song ", written by Joseph Harvey at Lowestoft, while doing duty there with

the Halesworth Loyal Volunteers in 1804; as I
started my own Volunteer services at Halesworth
just eighty years later, when they were still going
strong there, I would like to include one verse of
Private Harvey's rather poor stuff for the sake of
Auld Lang Syne.

" Attend Lowestoft Fair, I pray,
    And banish vain affright;
    We come to laugh with you by day,
    And guard your coast by night."

Chorus. " Then sleep dear Girls, at love's command,
        Nor dream of Gallia's roar;
        While we, the guardians of our land,
        Are watching on your shore."

During the 1860 Volunteer revival Rifle Corps
were again established all over Suffolk, and drilled
with the old muzzle-loading Enfield Rifle, a
weapon, which if well loaded, was apt to kill at
both ends.

The Wrentham Corps were practising volley
firing with blank and Private Smith, who was a
bit timid, kept on loading, but never fired, propos-
ing to draw the charges after drill; however they
went on to file firing, and presently it came to his
turn. " Now then Smith," roared the Instructor,
" Fire away ", so Smith shut his eyes and pulled
the trigger; with a shattering blast the rifle flew
over his shoulder, down went Smith, and as he

fell he shouted to his comrades " Look out together, she ha' got to goo orf seven or eight times more yet."

An old friend being in Edinburgh on some occasion, a long time back, went to see the castle, and up on the terrace he came on a lovely Highlander on sentry go, togged out in all the Scottish panoply of war ; by inadvertence my friend went on to some forbidden ground, whereupon the Highlander stopped him, and said, " Yaou marn't goo there." Instantly my old Suffolk friend retorted, " Where d'yaou come from Bor ? " and that glorious Highlander replied " I come from Bungay."

Another soldier tale, but of the late War, was told me by a late officer of the Battalion ; the C.O. of the Suffolks was going round the trenches in France one night, when suddenly a Tommy tumbled over the parapet down into the trench at his feet. The C.O. said " Hullo ; where do you come from ? " and the man replied, " About fower mile tother side o' Bury St. Edmunds."

Another War time story I heard was told, rightly or wrongly, of Major General Egerton inspecting a Suffolk Battalion. Coming to a squad at aiming drill he asked a recruit " Why do we generally fire at six o'clock ? " I must explain that an instructor speaks of the target as a clock, the bullseye being the centre, and aim is taken at some selected hour round the clock face, most frequently six o'clock to allow for the rifle throwing high ; this budding marksman cheerfully replied " Cos thass tew dark at saven."

Heard in a Suffolk village one morning probably in 1916, " That was a good tidy owd Zellepin raid we had larst night."

There used to be a hardy joke about the South-wold Railway, called by visitors " the Toy Railway," to the effect that it was made for China, and sent out there, but returned because the Chinese wouldn't have it.

Now plenty of fun grew on the Southwold Railway tree without inventing branches to it, so I will explain how it was this fairy tale arose.

Ransomes, of Ipswich, supplied the engines, and metals, for the Shanghai-Woosung Railway, which was of 2 ft. 6 in. gauge, and was built in 1876, they also sent out one of their men, W. G. Jackson, to drive the engines ; these were happily named The Flowery Land, The Celestial Land, and The Pioneer, and Jackson actually drove the first train in China.

The Southwold Railway engines, and metals of 3 ft. guage, were also supplied by Ransomes, and were named Blyth, Halesworth, and Wenhaston, a fourth, named Southwold, was purchased later; that railway was commenced in May, 1878, and opened on the 24th September, 1879, and Jackson returned from China to drive those engines, and remained in charge of them until he retired to Reydon, where he died some years since, and did he not name his bungalow in Station Road, Southwold, " Shanghai Cottage," and that's all there is to it.

It will be obvious that 2 ft. 6 in. engines, and carriages, would not travel on a 3 ft. road.

I went home for the Christmas holidays via the new Southwold Railway in 1879, and I was a passenger by it the day before it closed in April 1929, being snapped for the pictures on that occasion.

I was a traveller by it when the engine ran off the metals between Wenhaston and Blythburgh, and I used to relate that we all got out and lifted it on again, but, to be strictly truthful, all we did was to pull down, and break up the fence to provide packing for the traversing jack with which the men worked her back on to the rails.

Some fifty years ago I travelled in one of the long thirds from Blythburgh, which was packed full, and I was the only one who was not a fisherman. My greeting was " Hullo, Master Arnie, you're in a rough lot this time," and what a cheery hearty crowd they were; one of the smartest was Freddy Etheridge, who jumped overboard to save a comrade, and gave his own life with his friend;

now I believe not a man goes fishing from that district.

Wright, the guard, told me at the time, of the young visitor who, missing the first train at Southwold one morning, ran along the line and caught it at Walberswick, but he qualified it by adding " we had some bit of shunting to do that morning." I always thought it hard that the man who beat the train should be prosecuted, and fined, for trespass.

I saw the line washed away several times, and on one occasion I sailed in my gun-punt over the line, in one part, and rowed under the hanging metals, in another place where the embankment was gone.

One Easter time, about 1880, when I was home for the holidays, we heard a pack of hounds, and rushing out saw Chaston pounding past the Lodge with a few couple of hounds and three or four horsemen, after an outlying deer; my brother jumped on a horse and joined in, but no other horse being at home I had to stay behind; the deer and hounds crossed the River Blyth near the new Railway Bridge, and there being then no Pontoon Ferry, the nearest way over was Blybro Bridge, eight miles round, so the Hunt decided to risk the Railway Bridge, and pulling down a rail or two they got on to the line, and safely led their horses over the bridge, and on to the marshes by Southwold Common.

But a " fule " from Blyford Queen's Head, who has been an angel many a year, must needs drive

along the line with a pony and cart ; when he got
to the Bridge it was only planked between the
metals, 3 ft. wide, the rest being open cross timber
work, however Jehu was not to be gainsaid, and
he enlisted the help of two men to walk on the
plankway, behind the cart, and carry the back
of it, while he led the pony in front ; and so the
procession started, and had safely navigated half
the crossing, when the demon of cussedness
arranged for the Southwold Express to arrive, and
be stopped by this queer concern on its bridge.

When the pony and cart were over the bridge
they could not be got over the ditches, and had to
be assisted along the railway to the Common
Gate ; altogether the train must have been delayed
half an hour, and the wrath of the mighty was
great.

The deer was taken in the sea at Easton, but
that did not end the story, for the ponycart hunts-
man was prosecuted, and smartly fined, and then
he went round with the hat to all the others who
crossed before him, and I believe it cost them about
a guinea apiece.

An old sea captain friend of mine finished his
days near the Southwold Station Yard, and when
getting childish, at something over eighty, he went
one day with the linen line, and moored the engine
to one of the trees growing on the platform.
" There ye are together," said he to the driver and
fireman, " she's all right now, and you can go
below and smook your owd pipes."

Now I fear those engines are moored in the " comdemned hole " as sailors call a ship's grave-yard, and so passes the Southwold Railway.

My mother was born in 1827, and she might possibly have heard this story she used to tell us of the old clerk, at Bradwell I believe, or she may only have got it second hand ; but anyway on some occasion of the King's return after an absence, the clerk gave out in church :

> " King William has come home, come home,
> King William home has come,
> So let us sing to the glory of God,
> The Hymn thass called Te Dum."

She also related that she heard an old neighbour get up in church and forbid his daughter's banns ; another of her church stories was of Blythburgh days, when they sat and waited nearly an hour for the Rev. Blackman, then a messenger arrived, and the ancient clerk mounted the reading desk and announced, " There on't be no sarvice to-day, Master can't catch the powney."

The same clerk, old Esau Elmy, had a hook on one arm which I used to think was specially provided to fit the organ bellows handle ; on one occasion Esau asked my mother to excuse his rather mouldy appearance, for, said he, " I 'a jest come out o' the grave."

After farmhouse hospitality one frequently heard, " Thank ye for me Maam," or " Thank ye for me and mine," and we used to have a saying, " Thank ye for me and mine, and if ever you, and yours come to see me, and mine, I hope me, and mine will make you, and yours, as comfortable as you, and yours, have made me, and mine," but I cannot say that I ever heard it used seriously.

However I remember an old neighbour saying, " No Maam, no, M'arnt didnt give that to M'uncle, that was M'uncle gave that to M'arnt," and for ever after we knew him as " Munkle."

On another occasion I heard a Suffolk orator come out with this priceless harangue on the subject of infectious diseases :

" Where do all these here diseases come from ? Why they are browt into the town in the summer time ; we get Jack Ragtag, and Bobtail, and nobody know whew, from nobody know where, bringing millions o' miscrobes into the place, and what happens to them there miscrobes when they get into our bewtiful pure sea air ? Why, they EXPLODE, and us poor pesbyterians passin by get smothered with 'em, and catch all mander o' diseases."

Another of the same fraternity told me one day that he " shue " a lady, and children, all over his job and " splained " everything to them, took half an hour, and more, and then " She say to me ' Thank you very much ' she say. So I says, ' Maam,' I says, ' Thank ye's aren't no use to me, I 'a got a chist at home right full o' thank ye's.' She give me half a crown."

An old pilot friend, after I had entertained him one evening solemnly gave me the following bit of advice at parting : " When you are reefing taups'ls in a gale o' wind, you keep in the bunt, and let someone else go out, and pass the earring." I thought it rather useless advice to a landlubber but no doubt he meant it in a figurative sense, and that if I ran up against a nasty job in life I was to take the safe end of it.

———

When the Southwold train started, and the place got better known, an old lady who lived in a tiny two-roomed cot on one of the Greens, was observed to be very busy one morning, tarring the bottom courses of bricks, whitewashing the front, etc. ; a neighbour watched this until she could not bear it any longer, and so went across, and said, " Why, Mrs. Finney, whatever is up ? " " I'm a goin to let," was her reply. The neighbour, knowing well there was only one tiny room below, and a smaller one over, enquired with interest what she was going to let. " Why," said Mrs. Finney, " I'm a goin to set up and let the bed."

———

The maid brought in the tea all right but when her mistress began to pour out, only hot water came from the spout, so she rang, and said " Why Emily you forgot to put in the tea." " Reelly Maam," said Emily, " well I am sorry, I don't know how I come to forget it," and took the pot away to make it properly, but at the door she turned back to say, " Why now I remember why I didn't put in the tea, there air noon."

———

" COOTIN " IN SUFFOLK

———

John and Mary were sitting some distance apart on a stile, and getting on very slowly :
Mary : Don't scruge me so John Bor.
John : I bain't a scrugin on you Meary.
Mary : You might if you liked John Bor.

———

Another couple had walked a mile or two without a word :

She : Bain't you a goin to spake John Bor.

He : I hain't nothin to say.

She : You might saay you love me John.

He : I 'a said that ariddy.

She : Well, you might kiss me John Bor.

He : That'll dew when we're married.

———————

There was a law case about a right of way along a certain creek wall, and the oldest inhabitant was giving evidence :

Judge : You say you have seen couples on this wall, what were they doing there ?

Methusalah : They were jugglin.

Forby says to " Jug " is to nestle close together like partridges at night, and we may imagine that Meary would be saying to John, " Now then ha' done you'll spile my bonnet."

———————

Overheard in the Waveney Valley train :

" Pulham Meary, Pulham Meary ; that allus maake me laarf that dew ; that mind me o' pullin Meary Smith about."

MOTORING DIRECTIONS

" Dew—yaou goo as fur as Wiggses farm, then tarn agin tew haystacks, then howd to the left, past the parson's, down a hill, over the bridge, then taake the second rood to the right, and if yaou keep a goin right, yaou carn't goo wrong."

VIII

THE BACKUS BOY

Thass saventy year come harvest time,
Since I fust went ter wark,
An' tarned my hand ter ivery thing
From arly morn till dark;
An went bahdsnazing in the spring,
Wen all the holls were green,
An' in the Nuttery look ter find,
Hay Jack and Titty Wreen;
      Wen I w're a Backus Boy.

King Harrys allus used ter build
In a gret owd hulver tree,
An' if no eggs w're in a neast,
" Thass fit for an egg," says we.
Them Mavishes and Fulfers tew
Would sing a luvily tune,
An' that owd cuckoo he'd begin
A huckering come June,
      Wen I w're a Backus Boy.

The Hornpipes flew quaverin round,
Wen I went down the Fen,
For kindlin, but them wipers there,
They wholly scared me then;

Come winter ther'd be troshin days,
An' I'd kill rats and meece,
Till Missus used ter hollar, " Boy ;
Ha' you shet up them geese ? "
  Wen I w're a Backus Boy.

Wen barley in the barn they'd stack,
I used to ride the goof,
Round an' round, my hoss an' I,
Until we reached the roof ;
And then the min would make a slip,
In the corn agin the side,
And pull, and shuff owd Smiler in,
Plump to the ground he'd slide.
  When I w're a Backus Boy.

An' if my hands w're blue wi' cowd,
An' my close were dreepin wet,
Our Missus she would ax me in,
An' by the fire I'd set,
Ter git my wittles in the warm,
A rare good hearted one,
An' sometimes bakin days she'd say,
" Catch Johnny, there's a bun."
  Wen I w're a Backus Boy.

Ah, Bor, the games we used to hev
In the Backus arter dark,
For the mawthers up at sarvice there
W're master fond of a lark ;

But one night I were tittlin one,
Wen she shruck out " Oh Lord,"
Our Master he come boltin in
An hulled me out abroad ;
   That done me for Backus Boy.

So then I made the woyages,
The North Sea, Home and Spring,
In them there Half and Halfer botes,
Till I gin my gal a ring ;
The next I took a hossman's place,
An' went ter plough all day,
We used ter tarn our hosses with
Whoyeesh, an' Cuppywhey,
   Wen I w're a good full man.

Come harvest time a cartin waate,
We'd take the fild across,
An' hollar wen a shock was pitcht
" Howd ye ! Goo on owd hoss, "
But now I'a wrowt my innards out,
An' can't dew nothin more,
I set an' think o' them owd times,
For things ain't nothin what they wore
   Wen I w're a Backus Boy.

IX

MISTRESS MARY NEALE

In the latter half of the seventeenth century one
Thomas Neale owned a seat about a mile from
Bramfield Church, which, according to the Hearth
Tax Return of 1674, was the largest house in
Bramfield, having nine hearths; more than one
hundred and fifty years ago this seat was converted
to a farmhouse, and I believe has since been pulled
down. Mr. Neale died in 1704, aged fifty-three,
and was buried in Blythburgh Church, with his
father and grandfather; by his will he provided
for the erection of almshouses at Bramfield, and
for six poor children to be taught to read the Bible,
and his widow, Mary, supplemented the gift by a
legacy of £100; the almshouses were erected in
1723, and the charity is still alive. Neale was
evidently a man of position in the Parish, and
County; he was churchwarden in 1654 and 1669,
and in the churchwardens' accounts for 1685 is
the following entry, " To Thomas Neale Esq. for
the Leete ffee, 12.2."

Suckling records that he was one of the best
magistrates in his time, and he was possibly a
lawyer by profession, and steward of the Courts

Baron and Leet; he also evidently had a leaning towards the Dissenters created by James II, for in 1695 he figured with Sir Robert Rich, of Roos Hall, Beccles, and Samuel Pacey, of Lowestoft, as one of the first trustees of the Lowestoft Dissenting Chapel built that year. Pacey was I believe, the grandfather of the Pacey girls who figured in the famous Lowestoft Witch Case, see " Witchcraft in Suffolk," post. Neale by his will also gave a rent charge of £2 10s. per annum, for the purpose of teaching five poor children of Blythburgh to read, and 10s. a year for buying Bibles for young persons there, and this charity is also still in being; from this, and from the fact that their family tomb is in the chancel of Blythburgh Church I assume that the family were formerly resident at Blythburgh, but so far I have not found any other record of them there. A pedigree is at the British Museum, Add. MSS. 19143.

This was therefore a kindly man, attached to children and interested in their education and spiritual welfare, and Bramfield and Blythburgh should both treasure his memory. He had only one child of his own, a daughter, Mary, born 1684, and had the great misfortune to lose her at the early age of ten. To give an idea of the dour, puritan, attitude towards the beliefs and creed of little children in those austere dissenting days, let me quote from the sermon preached at her funeral, at Blythburgh Church, by the Rev. Joseph Fenn, Vicar of Sibton, and quondam Vicar of Reydon

with Southwold, on the 3rd July, 1694, of which
I happen to have a copy:

At the close he speaks of " a pleasant Flower
taken off in the Bud by the Hand of Death,
authorized by a Divine Commission," and relates
that, " When Death made near approaches, and
she apprehended the time of her departure at hand,
she shewed more than ordinary willingness to die.

" Being asked Whether she were willing to leave
her Father and Mother, and all the expectations
of an only Child? She replied, *I am willing to leave
them all, to go to God, to Glory, to Heaven;* One
enquiring of her, what Ground she had for her
hope of Salvation? She returned this Answer,
*In and through the Merits of Christ I hope to obtain
Salvation.*

" When some Questions were moved to her
concerning the Future State, the Enquirer received
such fitting Answers, as being unexpected from her
years, led them that were present into no little
Admiration; Being asked what she would have?
She answered, *Nothing but Death;* lifting up her
Hands and Eyes, said, *Come, Lord Jesus, come
quickly.*"

What a deathbed scene; what torment for that
tender kiddie of ten; catachized, before a crowd,
on matters that might have stumped a Doctor of
Divinity at such a moment, no wonder the poor
little soul longed for death; Mary has lain in her
tiny grave in the Chancel of Blythburgh Church
nearly two hundred and fifty years, under a slab

which records that she " with a Strain of Piety,
far beyond her Years, and a Chearfulness to
Admiration, humbly resigned her Soul into the
Hands of her Redeemer." But one cannot help
feeling the pathos of her last moments, and hoping
that she found the peace that passeth under-
standing.

This carries my mind back to my own father's
funeral at Blythburgh Church almost sixty years
ago, when I was even younger than Mary Neale ;
on a glorious June day, such another perhaps as
the 3rd July, 1694, but with the lugubrious pomps
of a mid-Victorian funeral, he also was laid to
rest in that peaceful, hallowed spot.

X

THE HALF AND HALFER ON A
BLOWING NIGHT

THE long glass in the bar stood at 28.8, and still falling. This pattern of a century and more ago had served its time at sea, and so would be used to bad weather ; if you looked about a foot down the case you could see the little brass socket in which the gimbal worked, and a brass bowl at the bottom which held lead ballast when it swung in the cabin of some well found ship, perhaps an East Indiaman.

In Holy Trinity, Bungay, is a stone to the memory of Capt. Thos. Stanton, of the good ship *Returne*, and it is there recorded that by his indefatigable industry he made a voyage to India and back in twelve months, fighting and beating a Dutch man-of-war on the way home, " the like not done since." Stanton died 1691, and as the barometer was invented in 1643 it is possible the *Returne* carried a primitive type of ship's barometer to help her captain to make the record round voyage to India which has long since been beaten out of sight.

Certainly the glass was not wrong for it was a dirty night, a heavy N.E. gale, and, with high water springs due about midnight, it promised to

be an anxious night for waterside dwellers on the
Suffolk coast.

The Half and Halfer fairly shook as the squalls
swept in from sea over the marsh lands, the rain
thrashed the windows at the back, and now and
again great clouds of smoke puffed out into the
bar, but all the same the few customers there
crowded close round the fireplace, gazing at the
yellow and violet flames from the old shipwreck
stuff, which Capt. Joe always provided for the
winter evening fire, when he could get it, and
harkening to the rumbling of the gale in the
cavernous old chimney.

It was one of those wild nights when seafaring
folk are restless, and cannot settle down indoors,
their instinct to face the gale, and defy the forces
of nature, seems on those occasions to bring out
some innate spirit of battle, and dogged resistance;
at such times the longshore man will keep going
out to have a look at it, to see how the tides are
working, or whether any of his brothers want a
hand with boat, or gear, and some will stand for
hours under the lee of a house, or lookout shed,
from whence a view of the sea, or harbour, can
be obtained.

I remember one who, when he lay dying,
insisted that the lifeboat was going off, and that
he must go and help launch her; he could only
be pacified by one of his friends who was brought
in to say that it had come on so thick with snow
they had given it up.

Another of my friends left his bride on his wedding night to go afloat in the lifeboat, and help save a crew in a snowstorm.

Some of them tramp for miles, with a small grappling, and a bit of cod-line, along the edge of the wave-swept beach, dark or daylight, poltering, i.e. on the look out for anything, from a bit of drift wood, to a ship's boat, or a man's body.

The Half and Halfer was built to stand this weather, long and low, with nothing much for the wind to get hold of, and the doorways placed high up to keep the raging tides out. You went up several steps, opened the door, and then descended on the inside to the road level again.

Many times the water had been a pane or two up the windows, when those inside could watch the little wavelets breaking up against the glass, accompanied by all the usual floating débris of a high tide.

It was necessary then to be ready with buckets, and handcups to bail out, and keep old Davy at a distance as long as possible ; but some times he would beat the humans, and rushing triumphantly in would drive them all to a higher level.

"Gaffer," said Capt. Joe, " if I were you I'd be agoin, the flood 'a got three hours good to run, and there'll be a heavy flow to-night, the people are getting their boats up on to the quay ariddy." Indeed one could hear them tramping about, and shouting to each other while they were making things secure, and it was all as good as the pictures to old Gaffer, who had been through it many times, and knew exactly what was going on although he was past lending a hand.

" Yes Captain," said he, " I suppose I must be agoin, but I'll give a toast fust," and raising his glass he looked round, and solemnly said, " All ships at sea." Everyone repeated " All ships at sea," and the Captain at the back of the settle, held his glass on high and completed the ritual by giving, " All ships in port." Hardly one of those present but had endured hardships, and dangerous times at sea, and, by way of compensation, enjoyed that sudden change to peace and security, following upon successful navigation into the shelter of a safe port.

> Safe home, safe home in port ;
> Rent cordage, shattered deck,
> Torn sails, provision short,
> And only not a wreck ;
> But oh ; the joy upon the shore
> To tell our voyage-perils o'er.

" Howd on Gaffer," said a fisherman, " afore you goo tell us that yarn about owd Pye and the ship ashore."

" Well, you must know," began Gaffer, nothing loth, " you've heerd of owd Peter Pye, him what had the Flyin Hoss years agoo, well when he give up the sea he got a way of dropping in every morning at Tink, the shumacker's shop, and havin a rest in his customer's chair, whiles they champed over the news of the day.

" Now Tink he had a regular rip of a boy then, up to all mander o' daviltry, he went for a sojer arterwards yer know, and got kilt, so this boy Tom he sneaked a bit o' cobbler's wax out 'n his father's tub, and warmed it up nicely by the kitchen fire, then he went and stood at the doer, whistlin like a innocent young cherubim, till he seed owd Capt. Pye a comin up the street ; then he slipped in after the wax, spreeded it on the seat o' the chair, and made orf out the backway.

" Well the owd Captain, he was ruptured yer know, and wery stiff on his legs, so he stiddies hisself a front of the chair and then lumped into it like a bag o' ballast, and they larnched orf about the wind, and so forth, cause there was a tidy breeze on ; by and bye when the wax had got nicely set, one o' Master Tom's chummies come running up and put his hid in. ' Ship ashore Captain,' he say, and cut away agin like mad.

" Up jumped the owd man, the chair with him ; he started to swear, the shumacker got howd o' the chair, and they pulled one agin the tother till there was a squakin, and a rendin, and the whole seat come out 'n his trousers, and away he started up the street as hard as he could goo, howdin his coat tails over the hole, and when he got to the clift o' course there worn't no ship ashore, nor no nothin ; lor they wholly mobbed him about that there, but I don't believe he iver found out whew done it."

"I wonder," said the young fisherman, when the laughter had subsided, "whether any on ye see that nottis in Tailor Thompson's window t'other day, that said in gret letters, ' Look here ; Thompson's Trousers down agin, 13s. 11d,' I thowt that worn't a bad un, but somebody must ha' got on ter him about it cos that was sune took down."

Just then the door opened and a boy appeared with a lantern. " Come on Granfer," said he, " Mawther ha sent me to fetch yer with a light, cos she say, haps you'd get led-will on a night like this." " All right," said the old man, " gimme my rockalow, and less be a goin," and so they helped the old boy on with his foul weather coat, and he made a start, but ran into a couple of stalwart, oil-frocked, sow-westered figures on the steps. " Cheeroh, owd Gaffer," says one, " what now orf home ? " " Yes," replied the ancient, " I'm sent for and so I'll goo and tarn in ; how dew she look on the front now ? "

" Well there's a lot o' wind still, and the sea run steeple-deep, they say thass a goin over the beach at the Nothe end ariddy, so we may be full up to-night if the tide run its time, goodnight " ; and Gaffer, and grandson departed while the new-comers descended into the bar and demanded a pint of warm beer apiece ; Mrs. Jentleman there-upon produced a large cone-shaped heater, and filling it with a quart from the cask, thrust the point well down into the fire, where in a very few minutes, it was hot enough to put a glow all through those stout hearts, and chilly extremities.

" I dunno why," said one of them, " but to-night fare to make me think o' that night we went after the *Decima*, what was a torchin orf the town. About twenty-five year agoo that was, but I was one of 'em that time, and when we got to her she was a proper wreck, topmast and spreet gone, and every stich o' canvas blown clean out on her, and dew you think them fallers would come out on her? not they.

" We went right alongside to get 'em, and a sea took us, and lumped our bote right on top o' the lee-board, smashed our pad to shatters, and started the deck planks, so we hollared to them to look sharp, for the seas were a goin right acrost her amidships, but she worn't so bad aither ind; the skipper stood in the hoodway aft and sung out she wornt makin no water, and he thought if he let goo his anchor she'd ride it all right till we could get a tug.

" We were then about three or four mile from the shore, and settin orf like all that, but they won't come out, and so we left 'em ridin there in the open sea and made for Lowestoft; we went in there about three in the mornin, and got the *Dispatch* as soon as we could. She took us in tow, and away we went agin, right in the teeth on it, to go out o' the Stanford.

" Goin through the Gat we took a full grown
sea that broke the towrope like a bit o' spunyarn,
but the tug sune picked us up agin, and by and
bye we browt the wind more aft, and most on us
got underneath the foresail, and went along a
little bit more comfortable.

" Howsever, when we got to where we left the
wassel, she worn't no where to be seen, and we
cruised up and down for an hour or more, till at
last we found her a ridin a good nine mile from
the land, and drivin orf into the sea like billy-oh ;
once we got to her that din't take us long to pass
the rope, and some of our chaps, what we put
aboard, slipped the cable, and we hung on astarn ;
I rackon that was about nine o'clock afore we got
her into Lowestoft, and my heart we put away
a funny brakfast when we got ashore.

" That was wery nigh a twenty-four hour job
afore we got home agin, and though the weather
was jest as bad as what that is to-night, we only
got £50 for it, and that was worth £100, whatever
more ; thass the worst of a tug, they allus want
to scorf the bloomin lot, we should ha' done better
to ha' took her to Harwich on our own, but you
see she was bound to Lowestoft, and the skipper
was set on gittin her there ; all the same I could
dew with another job like that to-night I could,
what say you owd Captain ? "

" Well," said the landlord, " what I say is,
when I was master of a ship I was glad to keep
clear o' you fellers. ' Longshore shurks ' we used

to call you, but now I'm ashore thass another thing, and the more jobs you get the better for all in a little place like this."

"Did I ever tell ye of that time we were assisted into Yarmouth, when I had the old *Jim Crow*, a hard headed old davil she was at the best o' times, and when one o' them clumsy collier boats cut acrost us, while we were a beating through the Roads, and took our bowsprit, and all the headgear, out, well I couldn't do nothing with her, and so I had to take a tug what come to us. I tried to make a bargain, but the skipper said no, we must settle it when we got in, and as we looked like going on the Scroby if we didn't do something right quick, I had to give 'em a rope and they tew us in.

"Well of course I couldn't do nothin with them shurks, and they made a law job of it, and my owners they put the steamboat people in the court too, so by-n-bye I, and old Harry Howsago, what was mate along o' me, had to go, and be witnesses, and when old Harry was called on the Judge say to him, sharp like, 'Well my man, who are you for? the plaintiff or the defendant?' 'I dunno,' says Harry, garping like a winded cod. 'Well,' says the Judge, 'you're a pretty fellow to come here to give evidence, and don't know who you are for, but never mind, tell us where you were when this collision happened.'

"'I were abaft the binnacle,' says Harry. 'Wait a minute,' says the Judge, 'where did you say you were?' 'Abaft the binnacle,' says Harry agin. 'Where-ever is abaft the binnacle?' says the old Judge. 'Well I never,' says Harry, right plump, 'you're a pretty judge to set here to judge this here case, and don't know where abaft the binnacle is'; lor, how that old Judge did laugh, and everybody else, and I do believe that helped us a lot cause he give the case agin the steamboat, and her insurance had to pay all our expenses, and the tug too, so we got out o' that very well.

"Now I wish one of you chaps would go and have another look at it, for I do believe the wind has drawed orf, and moderated a bit, and we don't want to be messin about half the night for nothin."

"All right Master," said one of the men, "I'll goo find out," and he stumped off, up and down the steps, and out into the night, to return in some minutes with the news that the tide was done, and the wind eased, and that there was no need to worry any further about it for this time, and so the landlord by way of a wind up gave them the old toast of "Two Ins and One Out, In health, In wealth, and Out of Danger." He then wished the company all a goodnight, and saw them safely off the premises, and so to bed very sober.

XI

SOME PILGRIM FATHERS FROM SUFFOLK

On the 14th January, 1611, there was instituted to the Vicarage of Reydon, " cum capella de South-wold," the Rev. Christopher Yonges, who was said to have been B.A. Oxford, and to have served as Chaplain of Windsor during Queen Elizabeth's reign ; he had several children, amongst them, Margaret, Christopher, Edward, Elizabeth, and John ; the last named was born about 1598.

Edward and Elizabeth were drowned in the haven on that sad occasion when twenty-two Southwold people lost their lives through their boat capsizing coming from Dunwich Fair, on St. James' Day, 25th July, 1616.

Agnes Strickland wrote a little story round this tragic event, entitled " Dunwich Fair," published I believe, in " All the Year Round," and she sets out verbatim the poor father's tear-stained record in the Southwold Church register, as follows :

" The names of those who were drowned and found again. They were drowned in the haven coming from Donwich Fayer, on St. James's day in a bote, by reason of one cable lying overwharf the haven, for by reason the men that brought them down was so negligent, that when they were redie to come ashore the bote broke lose, and so the force of the tide carried the bote against the cable and so overwhelmed. The number of them were xxii, but they were not all found. The widow Robson, Johne Bates, Mary Yewell, Susan Frost, Margaret Blackbourne and the widow Taylor, were all buried on the 26th day of July, being all cast away, coming from Donwich Fayer, on St. James's daye.

" Widow Foster was buried the 27th day of Julye, Bennett Allen was buried the 30th daye, Goodie Kerrison same daie. Edward and Elizabeth Younges, daughter and son to me C. Younges, vicar and minister, was buried the 31st Dae of Julie. All these were found again in this towne and buried."

The Rev. Christopher died on the 14th June, 1626, and lies buried in Southwold Church, no doubt in the chancel, where was formerly a brass with this inscription :

" HERE LYETH INTERRED THE BODY OF MR. CHRISTOPHER YONGES WHO DEPARTED THIS LIFE THE 14 DAY OF JUNE Ao Dni 1626.

" A Good man full of fayth was hee,
Here preacher of God's word,
And manie by his Ministrie
Weare added to the Lord. Acts, 11.24."

This brass has lately been moved about from place to place in the church, and is now fixed in the nave floor under the pulpit, where it is quite out of place. It should be restored to its matrix in the chancel, which no doubt marks approximately the spot where this " Good Man " lies.

John Yonges also became a minister, and was married on the 25th July, 1622, to Joan Herrington, née Jentilman, widow of Robert Herrington, to whom she was married 7th March, 1613 ; she was the daughter, I believe, of Wm. Jentilman of the Dunwich Family, so very well known in Suffolk shipping affairs in Tudor times, who migrated to Southwold in the sixteenth century.

The Rev. John Yonges made his home in Southwold for some years, and the register records the baptisms of two of his children, John on the 10th April, 1623, and Thomas on 1st May, 1625. His father died as we have seen in 1626, and his mother was buried at Southwold 5th November,

1630, which seems to be the last Yonges' entry. It is probable that the Rev. John left Southwold after his father's death, and in 1637 he is mentioned as of St. Margaret's Suffolk, when he was one of those ministers of whom it was said they were, " chased out of Old into New England for Non-conformity."

The examination list of those desirous to pass into New England by the *Mary Anne*, of Yarmouth, William Goose, Master, contains this entry: " May the 11th 1637. The examination of John Yonges of St. Margretts Suff., Minister, aged 35 yeares, and Joan his wife aged 34 yeares with 6 children, John, Tho., Anne, Rachell, Marey and Joseph ar desirous to passe for Salam in New England to inhabitt," but there is a marginal note against this entry, " This man was forbyden passage by the Commissionrs and went not from Yarmouth."

Another Southwold man examined was " William Cockram of Southold in Suff. Mariner ageed 28 yeares, and Christen his Wife ageed 26 yeares with 2 children, and 2 Sarvantes desirous to passe for new england to inhabitt."

Although forbidden to sail from Yarmouth John Yonges and his family arrived at Salem in the *Mary Anne*, and it is supposed that they crossed to Holland, very likely from Southwold, and joined her there; the examination list shews that several people went by the Mary Anne to Holland, so that she clearly called there on her passage.

It is on record that about the 14th August, 1637, he was received as an inhabitant, and afterwards granted land at Salem, but that he remained there only about one season, and a hard life it was we know ; later he removed to Long Island, to a place then known by its Indian name, " Yennycok." By 1649 it had received the name Southold, after the Suffolk town where their chief inhabitant, and pastor, was born, and it will be noticed the name is spelt in the same way as in the examination of Wm. Cockram of Southold (England).

Mr. Yonges' son, John, who we have seen was also born at Southwold, became a sea-captain, and on one occasion defended the Long Island settlements from the Indian Chief, Ninigret ; which reminds one of Max O'Rell's famous saying that when the Pilgrim Fathers arrived in the New World they first fell on their knees, and then upon the aborigines. Capt. John Youngs became one of the leading people in the new town of Southold, and was evidently a brave, capable, and reliable person, like many others of Suffolk stock.

The Rev. John's sister, Martha, baptized at Southwold, England, 1st July, 1613, also joined the little community with her husband Thos. More, and spent the rest of her life there ; his sister Margaret married Capt. Joseph Youngs, and they also settled at Southold for good. William Cockram, however, sailed from there for England on the 3rd October, 1642, his name then being spelt Cockrane, and probably returned to

his native place, as from 1667 onwards, Will.
Cockrain appears frequently in the list of bailiffs,
the name perhaps being carried on by a son.

The Rev. John Yonges died on the 24th
February, 1672, and upon his tomb, in Southold
Churchyard, is this inscription :

" Mr. John Yonges minister and first settler
of the chuch of Christ in Southhould on Long
Island deceased the 24 of February in the yeare of
our Lord 1672 and of his age 74.

" Here lies the man whose doctrine life well knowen
   Did shew he sought Crist's honour not his owen
   In weaknes sown in power raisd shall be
   By Christ from death to life eternally."

It will be noticed that his age here differs from
that given in the examination, and it is not clear
which is correct.

The house built by his son John, in 1647, is
still standing, and the history of the Youngs
family has been written by Selah Youngs, Jr.,
and published in New York, 1907.

Southold is now more than twice the size of
our Southwold, and is a prosperous and patriotic
little township, about one hundred miles from
New York. The association between the two has
been kept alive from time to time, and various
Southold citizens have been to visit our Suffolk
town and vice versa.

From the 21st to the 25th July, 1915, whilst we were in the midst of that terrible war, Southold celebrated its 275th Anniversary, and I may perhaps put on record the letter I wrote to the Celebration Committee on the occasion :

" Town Clerk's Office,
" Southwold, England,
" July 9th, 1915.

" Dear Sir,

" The attention of the Town Council of South-wold has been drawn to your letter of the 15th May with reference to the 275th Anniversary of your Town's Foundation, and I am directed by the Council to offer their hearty congratulations upon the occurrence of this very interesting event.

" The Council are particularly grateful for the kindly message of sympathy contained in your letter, which is specially welcome at this time of National peril and stress. This Town lies upon the East Coast within a few score miles of the scene of some of the heaviest fighting, and almost the whole of our efficient male population is serving either afloat or ashore.

" We look forward with confidence to a lifelong, and honourable peace and the freedom, and integrity, of small countries in whose defence England drew her sword.

" To return to domestic matters it may interest your Townsmen to know that two portions of the Sea front here are known as Long Island Cliff and New York Cliff, and there is no doubt these names were adopted when many of our ancestors emigrated to your district, and helped to found the Town of Southold.

"With every good wish for the success of the Celebration, and the prosperity and happiness of your Town, I am

"Yours sincerely,
"Ernest R. Cooper,
"Town Clerk.

"F. R. Mitchell, Esq.,
"Southold, New York, U.S.A."

The following persons went from Wrentham, Suffolk, in the *Mary Anne*, in May, 1637, viz., Thomas Paine, weaver, aged fifty, Elizabeth his wife and six children; John Thurston, carpenter, aged thirty, and Margaret his wife with two children; also Joane Ames, of Yarmouth, wydow, aged fifty years, with three children, Ruth, William, and John, who were connected with Wrentham in this way: Dr. William Ames, born at Ipswich, 1576, a well known Nonconformist, had a sister Elizabeth who married John Phillip, Rector of Wrentham, 1611. Ames was driven to emigrate to Holland, where he died in 1623, owing to a chill sustained when Rotterdam was inundated by the sea that year; his widow thereupon returned to Yarmouth with her three children, and in due course they went out with the Wrentham and Southwold people to Salem in the *Mary Anne*.

On arrival Mrs. Ames was granted land in Salem in 1637, and the same year the General Court voted " £40 to Mrs. Ames, the widow of Dr. Ames of famous memory." She died in New England in 1644; her daughter Ruth married out there, but William the son, after graduating, returned to England in 1644, and settled at Wrentham, where he later assisted his uncle John Phillip, as Co-Rector at Wrentham, and preached at Frostenden regularly; he also preached before the Lord Mayor at St. Pauls on the 5th November, 1651, and died at Wrentham 21st July, 1689. It is believed these people were the founders of Wrentham, U.S.A.

"Beniemen Cooper, of Bramton in Suffolk, husbandman, ageed fifty yeares," with his wife and five children, and others, also sailed in the *Mary Anne* for Salem. I cannot say what happened to them there, but I see a Thos. Cooper died in Southold in 1660, who may have been a relation.

Everyone, nearly, knows that John Winthrop, of Groton, Suffolk, the first Governor of Massachusetts, was a Suffolk man, born 1587-8 at Edwardstone in Babergh Hundred, died 1649; he led the great emigration to Salem in 1630, sailing on the 22nd March in the *Arabella* from Southampton for Salem.

It was through John Winthrop that so many Suffolk Puritans went to Salem, and New England, and he must have been a stout fellow in all ways as he had four wives and many children. The

Winthrops are said to have been Lavenham cloth-
workers, but they had long been settled at Groton,
where they were Lords of the Manor until John
sold it about the time of his renouncing Suffolk
to become Governor of Massachusetts. His father,
Adam Winthrop, left a diary of great local interest,
some extracts are contained in the *Bury Post*,
" Memorials of the Past," 1889.

John Winthrop is recognised as one of the
great men of his time in New England, and the
Massachusetts Historical Society has devoted much
labour to the study of his character and distinguished services in the early days of the colony.

Thomas Danforth (1622-99) was another Pilgrim
from Suffolk, who made good in the New World ;
he was the son of Nicholas Danforth, of Framlingham (who was a Juror of the Court Leet there
in 1629) and in 1634, at the age of twelve, Thomas
accompanied his father to New England and
settled at Cambridge, Mass.

Nicholas Danforth died 1638, but his son
prospered, and became first Treasurer of Harvard
College, Dep. Governor of Massachusetts, 1679-
1686, President of Maine, 1681-6, and a Judge
of the Court of Mass.

Thomas Danforth helped to found, and probably
gave the name to the Town of Framlingham,
Mass. He died at Cambridge, Mass., 5th November,
1699, and left twelve children to carry on the
family name and traditions.

Those who attended the pageant at Framlingham

last year will remember the Episode of Nicholas Danforth taking farewell of his native town, and Lord Howard, at the castle.

The more one looks into the records of Salem, Boston, Southold, etc., and the histories of John Winthrop, Pastor John Yonges, the Danforths, and others, the more one realizes, with regret, how much our England must have lost by driving these sterling old Puritans overseas in search of that religious freedom which has long since come to us.

Apart from the great emigration of dissenters there was another important movement taking place at that period of colonial development, viz., the departure of parties of adventurers for Virginia, and the New Plantations, as they were called by some, in search of fortune, and what Sir Nigel, in the White Company, would call " honourable advancement."

An outstanding figure amongst these adventurers was Thomas Warner, also of Framlingham ; he was the son of William Warner, of Framlingham and Parham, and I believe the grandson of Francis Warner, who according to the 1568 Subsidy List, was then the wealthiest man in Framlingham ; he was also armour keeper at the castle, and bailiff of the Hundred of Loes, 1558-1611.

Francis married Mary, the daughter of Sir Edmund Rous, of Henham Hall, and their grandson, Francis Warner of Parham, married Elizabeth, daughter of Sir John Rous of Henham ; this lady was the foundress, in 1736, of the admirable Warner Charity at Boyton, Suffolk ; the Warners of Suffolk flourished at Saxham, Wingfield, Framlingham, Cransford, Cratfield and Parham, and must have had some influence in the county.

Thomas started life as a soldier, and must have been brought up in the precincts, and atmosphere, of that great castle ; no wonder then that he is described as " a man of extraordinary agillity of body and a good witt," and that may be the reason he decided to try his fortune in the new land of adventure overseas ; he sailed, it is said, from Woodbridge, a statement I have been unable to verify, in 1623, with his wife Sarah, a Dorset woman, his son Edmund, aged thirteen, and a friend and neighbour in Suffolk, named Charles Jeafferson.

They sailed for Virginia but made the same landfall as Columbus, the West Indies, and forthwith landed on one of them, and founded there the English Colony of St. Kitts, or St. Christophers. When established both Warner and Jeafferson made voyages home, and returned with more colonists and stores, but they endured great hardships in the early days.

Amongst other enterprises this soldier captained a little privateer, which he called the *Gift of God*, and with her made various prizes.

In 1627 they allowed a French privateer's crew to join them, principally to assist them in defending themselves against the warlike Caribs, and, although this partnership led to constant trouble with the French, the settlement was held jointly by English and French until 1713 when it became wholly English, and so remains to this day.

Thomas Warner was knighted during his visit home in 1629, and died 10th March, 1648 ; he was buried in the churchyard of St. Thomas, Middle Island, near Brimstone Hill, under a flat tombstone which says :

" First Read, then weep when thou art hereby taught,
   That Warner lyes interr'd here, one that bought
   With loss of Noble bloud, the Illustrious name
   Of a commander—Greate in acts of Fame,
   Trayned from his youth in armes, his courage bold
   Attempted brave exploites, and Uncontrold
   By fortunes fiercest frowns hee still gave forthe
   Large Narratives of Military worth,
   Written with his Sword's point, but what is man."
                              (rest partly illegible)

Sir Thomas' sons succeeded him worthily in the West Indies, and it is said some of his descendants still hold property in the Islands.

Charles Jeafferson, the friend and neighbour of Thomas Warner, also prospered in St. Kitts, and established a plantation there ; he paid several visits to England, and his son Christopher was born over this side in 1650.

After his father's death Christopher paid his first visit to St. Kitts to enter upon his inheritance ;

he sailed from London in February, 1676, in the *Jacob and Mary*, and a lively and entertaining account of his voyage and life in the island, contained in a series of letters written from there, 1676-1686 has been published in " A Young Squire of the 17th Century," London, 1878.

The Jeafferson pedigree is to be found in the Additional MSS. at the British Museum, No. 19137 ; the name appears in the records of Framlingham Woodbridge, Melton and Wickham Market, and several of that name were supporters of the recent Framlingham pageant.

XII

DIVERSIONS OF A DISTRICT VISITOR

VERY few get closer to the home life of the people than those kindly souls who sacrifice their time, sometimes their health, and often their peace of mind, in attending to the wants, and listening with sympathetic ear, to the troubles of their cottage friends.

So upon an imaginary representative of that devoted band of sisters, whom I will label " D.V." I will father these few stories, in illustration of the quaint, and unconscious humour, which often fell in their way in Suffolk; perhaps things are different now.

" Yes Miss," said an ancient dame, a regular attendant at the old village church, " the new Raverend ha' bin to see me, and so I says to him, ' Parson,' I says, ' would you be sa kind as to gimme a paou a little bit narer the pulpit ? 'Cos that there Mrs. Brown, and Mrs. Roberson, they set right afront o' me, and time yar sarmon treakle through them tew that dew fare most wunnerful poor stuff, that that raly dew.'

" And you may me believe Miss, he up, and out he went, and he never give nothin, *nothin* ; me dear, I was that stammed you might ha' knocked me down with a futher."

Calling upon a younger woman during the noon hour the D.V. found the children all at table, just finishing off their dinner, whereupon their mother addressed them thus :

"Now then, Howd yar tongues ; Ha' you together done yar wittles ? " "Yes Mawther," from the tribe. "Then sah for't.

And they gabbled off a grace, and out they rushed full of dumpling and steam.

Another poor soul who after suffering for long years from an " ugly tampered " and trying partner, had at last been left a widow, and was looking forward to drawing the pension, and enjoying the company and help of her children ; but it fell to the D.V. to take a message from the doctor and break to her that she had an incurable complaint, and could not expect to live very long.

" I think thass very hard Miss," said that patient creature, " very hard indeed to be taken orf like this after forty years of father."

Oftentimes the D.V. herself will receive some well meant advice, such as an old lady in the Alms House once offered.

"If iver you hev ter goo ter one o' them Horspitals Miss, don't you niver let them waash ye', they kilt my owd man a waashin on him. Why they not only waashed his hid, but they must waash his whull body, and that kilt him."

D.V. : But Mrs. Jessop your husband didn't die at the Hospital did he?

"Oh no Miss, I know he dint, he lived for werry nigh twenty years arter he come out o' there, but that kilt him."

———————

When one poor old chap was breaking up he would sit by the fire all day, and would hold his tummy, and wail "Oh prah dew lave orf a harf a minute, prah dew"; sometimes queer noises would come from his corner, and his good old wife would look at him and say to the D.V. "Ah pore dear, how his innards dew rumble about;" and her neighbour would say, "Ah, my husband ain't like that, he never wrowt his inside out when he was young."

———————

And that reminds me of a story of a Suffolk Hospital, in their early days. The Committee having decided to visit the wards occasionally to see if all went well, a retired Admiral put his head in the door of the Women's Ward one day, and bawled out, "Any complaints ; any complaints ? "

" Yis, Sah," said an old woman timidly, and the Admiral pounced on her fiercely.

" Out with it then my good woman, out with it."

" I carn't Sah, it's me innards."

And when several were watching the last flickers of life in a good old neighbour, " Ah," said one, " pore dear, she on't be long now, I knew dreckly I see her she was marked for death, about twalve o'clock I rackon she'll be in Beelzebub's bosom." " Hush, Martha," interposed another watcher, in a shocked whisper, " That worn't the gentleman's name."

Long ago I heard another queer tale which I think must have had a foundation of truth in far back days.

An old fellow died who had been married twice, and left a grown up family and a young childless widow ; he was to be buried at a distant parish, and, perhaps for that reason, it was arranged for the lawyer to read the will before the funeral.

So the family were all assembled in the parlour, including a garrulous old Mrs. Gamp, who called herself a " Nuss," and had done for the deceased at the last ; whilst they were waiting she informed them what a dear, kind old gentleman he was, and would never give her any trouble, and would always get out of bed, right up to the last, and was so grateful, and how she was sure he would leave everything all right.

Presently the will was read, and it appeared he had left almost everything to the children, the widow came off badly, and the "Nuss" was not mentioned at all ; then a change set in, the widow became hysterical, and Mrs. Gamp arose in her wrath, and denounced the testator for a "wicked owd willan, and a troublesome owd feller" and related how he would get out of bed when he was told not to, and didn't she let into him with a slipper.

"However," said she, "they shall never bury him if I can help it," and up she went and locked the chamber door, seated herself in front of it, and defied the undertaker and his men, so at last rather than have a piece of work with her, they sent for a carpenter who took the window out and the coffin was got down and carried off.

———

I heard another funeral story from a Mid-Suffolk village where they had the thrifty habit of keeping their dead till Sunday if possible, so as not to lose any time over the funeral.

A parishioner having died, a relative went to inform the parson, who was properly sympathetic, and then inquired when the funeral was to be. "Waal Sah," was the reply, "we kinder rackoned ter hev it o' Sunday."

Now the parson was getting tired of this custom, and said, "Well I'm sorry, but it's not convenient to me. Sunday is my busy day you know; two services and Sunday School, and you must make it Saturday." Whereupon the relative replied, "Waal Sah, if you carn't hev it o' Sunday o' course you carn't " . . . pause . . . "but we shall bring um."

D.V.: Morning Mary, I just looked in to wish you happiness for I hear you are going to be married; rather sudden isn't it?

Mary: Why yes Miss, that fare so, but you mind Mrs. Marbbs a dyin a time back?

D.V.: What Mrs. Mobbs at the Bridge Foot?

Mary: Yes Miss, you see Missis she give me leave to goo to the fewneral, and naow I'm a goin to marry Mr. Marbbs; he saay I wus the life and sowl o' the whull paarty that daay, and he ha' had his eye on me iver since.

Then there is another district visitor story, which may or may not belong to Suffolk, but I have told it, by request, so many times, and it goes so well in broad Suffolk that I have come to be quite sure of its local origin.

"Yes, Miss, my pore owd dear is gone, he dint last long after you were here, and y'know when he laid so bad doctor he sent him a bottle o' physic, and that was marked to be took in a *re*cumbent *po*sition.

"And y'know Miss, I hain't got one, so I goes in to my neighbour and I says, ' Mrs. Jones maam,' I says, ' my owd man is mortal bad, and doctor he ha' sent him some physic, and thass to be took in a *re*cumbent *po*sition, and y'know I hain't got one. Ha' you got one ? ' And she says, ' No,' she say, ' I hain't got one, but I know hew hev, leastways she had if she hain't made orf with it, and thass Mrs. Brown down at the White Hoss.'

"So down I goes to the White Hoss, and I says, ' Mrs. Brown maam,' I says, ' my poor husband is a layin bad, and doctor he ha' give him a bottle o' physic to be took in a *re*cumbent *po*sition, and you know I hain't got one, and my naybour, Mrs. Jones, she hain't got one, but she say she believe you ha' one. Is that right ? ' And Mrs. Brown she say, ' Yes,' she say, ' I ha' got one, but I ha' lent it out, and thass over to Wrentam,' she say, ' but there, niver you mind if I be alive and well, I send my little boy for it in the morning.'

"And d'you know Miss, when that boy went the next d'mornin, that woman had lorst it, and so I niver could give the pore owd dare that physic, and I ha' got the bottle now if you'd like to see it."

———————

"Good afternoon Mrs. Deek, here's a lovely day, and do you know what day it is? Why it's Waterloo Day, you know, the day the Duke of Wellington beat the French."

"Dessay Miss, and now I come to think on it I've heerd my owd man talk about when we fowt the Frenchmin, and gained the day ; Sim tell the lady about when we hided the Frinch at that battle o' Waterloo."

"Why sartinly," said Sim. "I know all about the battle o' Waterloo, why that was fowt in Ben-acre Park that was."

D.V. : Well I hardly think that Mr. Deek, it was fought over the water you know.

Sim : Oh no Miss, beggin yar pardon, I know thass right what I say 'cos my mother she towd me so, and she was a tidy mawther when that happened, an' more be token, there's a place now in Benacre Woods, what they call the Blood Pit, where the sowdjers was buried arterwards.

D.V. : I daresay there was a battle fought there when the Danes used to come and land about here, but that was a thousand years ago.

Sim : Well Miss I hain't got the larnin to argufy along o' you, and don't know great A from a bull's foot, but thass what my owd mother towd

unto me, and I dunno what call she had to tell
me a lie; she said they used to sing:

" The Frinch are a comin, Oh dear, dear, dear,
  A lot of owd min that goo sneer, sneer, sneer;
The Frinch are a comin, Oh lork, lork, lork,
  A lot of owd women goo talk, talk, talk."

D.V.: I was sorry to hear you weren't well
Jethro, so I just looked in to see how you were
getting on.

" Thank ye Miss, I fare a little batter to-day, I
was took bad on Saturday when I was at work;
suffin struck me inside, and they had to carry me
up home; I had tew gret long pains, as long as
yer arm, and twenty or thirty little ones no longer'n
that," indicating the first joint of a finger, " but
my Missus she rubbed me well wi' Hoss Oils,
and that put me all of a muck wash; I 'a got the
tarn of it now, but that put me into a proper frap
at fust, I thowt I was a dunner and was a goin
to be like her what dropped dead last week, you
knew her dint ye? Owd Sally down o' Love
Lane. Blue nosed Sally we used to call her; she
was a orfspring she was, you know Miss, one o'
them onfortnit ones; no father, but a good owd
gal for all that.

" But I tell ye what Miss, hare I lay, and don't
know nothin, we 'a bin married forty years, and yet
my wife carn't tell me which way the wind blow.

How is the wind this mornin Miss ? That look wunnerful tempestified to me and if the wind be orf that 'll tarn up squally arter high water time, see if it don't."

Old folk always disparage the rising generation, and I have woven together a few of the criticisms I have heard at different times as a sample and trust the " mawthers " will forgive me for making fun of some of them.

List to Mrs. Lumpkin, of Lumpus Lane :

" Lawkadaisy, drat if that gret slammikin mawther o' mine hain't now fell soshways acrost the throshold, and broke the gotch.

" What the gals air a comin to I don't know, why what d'you think ? The t'other day I went to take my husband his fourses in the harvest fild, so I had to goo tro the yards ; I see the Missis stand at the wash killer in the backus, along o' the gal, but what d'you think ' Miss ' 'Melia was a dewin ? Why I heerd her a troshin the puny in the Drorin room 'stids o' hopin har mother, and she wore as thin as a yard o' pumpwater ; I'd give har puny I would, a lazy little muck.

" An' look at the close they wear, right down ondacent I call 'em ; they tell unto me thass the War what done it, and gals allus goo so arter a war, but I don't know ; what dew they want to paint their faces up for ? 'Strus I'm alive I see a

mawther the t'other day, and she'd enough flour
on har face to make a poor man a good dumplin ;
a lot o' silly bold critters a flyin about with chaps
on them motorbikes.

"And yet my naybour she say to me, she say,
'Let the gals alone Libby,' she say, 'they are
havin a rare good time. I wish things had a bin
like they are when I was a gal.' So there ye are,
some o' the mothers are as bad as the gals."

XIII

SHIP NAMES ALONG THE SUFFOLK COAST

WHAT a fund of interest would be attached to the old-time ship names if we could but recover a little of the history of the craft which bore them, and the men who manned them, and took a pride in what a modern steamboat hand would call Noah's Arks.

Ship names in themselves are a study, and a glance back shows that there were fashions in them as in most mundane things. The Vikings favoured names of a predatory type, such as *Long Serpent*, *Blue* or *Red Dragon*, *Raven*, *Vulture* or *Bison*, which accorded well with their bloodthirsty nature ; our own early ship names appear very eccentric to us, and it is difficult to explain such thirteenth century names as *Galopine*, *Belchere*, *Waynpayne* and *La Squinkin*; then the fashion tended towards religious names, and medieval days give us ships called *The Holy Ghost*, *The Ship of God*, *Petite Jesus*, *The Grace of God*, *La Trinitie* and so forth.

The Tudors gave us the first of those inspiring names, many of which have been repeated again and again in our navy, such as *Mary Rose*, *Thunderer*, *Dreadnought*, *Garland*, *Triumph*, *Nonpareil*, etc. The Stuarts, with their wonderful ships, in which the shipwright's decorative art reached its highest note, gave us many historic names, for example, *Revenge*, *Loyal London*, *Vanguard*, *Victory*, *Royal Oak*, *Britannia*, *Resolution* and so forth.

The Roundheads planned to commemorate their victories by calling their ships *Naseby*, *Basing*, *Fairfax*, *Marston Moor* and *Newbury*, but as may be supposed one of Charles II's first acts was to change all those names, and they have never been repeated.

The eighteenth century shews a quaint fashion in ship names, when many, chiefly privateers and slavers, were known as *Pretty Peggy*, *Charmin' Nancy*, *Lovely Betty*, *Little Billy*, *Sturdy Beggar*, etc. While a little later appears a run of classic names in the merchant fleet, such as *Diana*, *Juno*, *Pallas*, *Ceres*, *Atalanta*, which remained in favour for many years. The commercial instinct then cropped up, and was represented by *Industry*, *Leghorn Trader*, *Diligence*, *Enterprise*, *Farmers' Adventure*, and many similar names, while one hundred years ago our trading ships adopted the homely old English Christian names, especially of the owners' women-kind, and some of them were terribly overworked, for the 1843 Lloyds List gives one hundred and one *Marys*, eighty-nine *Janes*, and eighty-one *Anns*, while amongst men's names *William* holds the record with sixty vessels so called.

When one of these old wooden vessels went down at sea or came ashore, the oaken board, with the name and perhaps port, almost certainly came adrift to be picked up later by some long-shoreman, and nailed over the door of the finder's " Shod."

In my early days these boards and figure-heads were outstanding features of the Suffolk coast villages, and although many have disappeared, there are still a good few left for those who look around, and the fancy took me recently to note down what I could of those remaining before they also fade away, like the longshore fishermen themselves who are fast dying out ; last year a Hastings fisherman told me he had four sons, and not one would go fishing, or help him in his old age.

I was pleased to read recently in the *East Anglian Daily Times* that, although the Old Company of Lowestoft had been wound up, their watch hut, or storehouse, on the North Beach, had been taken over by the Sea Scouts for their headquarters, and that the figure-heads, and ship's nameboards, which have adorned it so many years, are likely to be preserved a little longer ; amongst the names there remaining are *John Pedder*, *James and Henry*, *Edward Kenny*, *Agathe*, and I am sure that some romance, or tale of shipwreck and daring rescue, attaches to several of these relics of a bygone age, and I hope I may hear a little about them from some who may read this.

Two or three figure-heads, and a good few nameboards are still left at Southwold, but I have been unable to recover much of the history of the older ones ; the good old homely *Betsy* bears signs of considerable age, but its grizzled owner could only tell me his father had it, and used to say she was lost at sea; in an old diary kept by James Maggs, of Southwold, 1797-1890, there is a note that the *Betsy*, Robert Wollage, master, was wrecked on Southwold Beach on the 19th May, 1791; is it possible that this may be her board, still going after one hundred and forty years? That old diary records constant wrecks on our exposed coast in those days.

Era is on an adjoining shed, and may be the relic of an old Whitby brig of that name; then the *Belle Isle*, one of the last of the once well known Shoreham brigs, and well remembered here, her crew having been rescued by the Southwold life-boat in 1873, and because her bottom still lies the other side of Dunwich Bight, and is a trap for trawl gear.

Spectator and *Royalist* are two good names, still defying the North Sea weather, but nothing is remembered of the ships which once bore them; in 1833 there was a *Royalist Brig* in the Royal Navy. *Rosebud* is all that is left of an old brig, once well known along our coast, in which a Southwold man served his time, and which was wrecked on Sole Beach forty or fifty years ago.

Now we come to a dilapidated old place decorated with the name *Billy*, a still well remembered ancient brig, hailing from Whitby, which at the age of fifty-five was lost with all hands off Southwold on the 15th January, 1866; the lifeboat made three attempts at rescue, but was swept past the wreck each time by the heavy sea; the *Billy's* crew were drowned one by one, and all that now remains is the name board perhaps one hundred years old.

Next is a foreigner, *Nord Havet*, a Norwegian bark, beached off Southwold in May, 1887, coal loaden and waterlogged; then a fine, well kept board, spreading well beyond the gable of its hut, displays *Nyl Ghau* to the curious eye, and its late owner was wont to relate that a gentleman told him it was Chinese for blue cow; then the homely name *William* figures on the front of a ricketty old place, but nothing could be gleaned of either of these except that they were picked up alongshore, and the same must be said of *Perkins, Grasmere* and *Concord*, which still remain more or less battered.

Britannia was the name of a North River wherry which finished its days as a mudcraft at Southwold, and in my possession are the boards of the *Cynthia*, a once famous racing yacht, built by Wanhill, of Poole, in 1849, of which a fine plate exists, now quite valuable, and which ended as a North Channel pilot cutter belonging to the pilots stationed at Southwold; *Refuge* is all that is left of an old Scarboro' yawl, built in 1862, which fished out of Yorkshire ports for some thirty years, and then carried coals to Suffolk until she was broken up just before the War, and finally in my hall hangs a more modern board with *Astrologer* deeply cut in it, this came ashore during the War, and was reported but nothing was ever heard by me as to the fate of that ship.

Over a cottage door, up a yard, in Victoria

Street is displayed the name board of the Norwegian bark *Idun*, which was wrecked at Southwold, 17th January, 1912, and whose story I told in my " Suffolk Coast Garland " ; I am told that the fife-rails from her quarter deck now serve as altar rails in Woodbridge School Chapel.

Further south on Dunwich Beach the name of the *Flora* will be seen on a shed used as a tearoom, and abreast of Sizewell House stands a lofty boathouse around which are fixed the following nameboards, *Pederaneus*, *Perseverance*, *Caroline*, *Lowestoft*, *Clarissa*, *Prudentia* and *Doune Castle*, and like those on the Lowestoft Hut I hope to learn something of their stories.

At Aldeburgh a number of nameboards used to be in the Lookout Huts, and when last there I noted the *Ruhtinas* and *Verveine* boards in the North Hut, but when I went to the other behold it had been turned into a teashop, and the guardian angel knew nothing of ship's nameboards, and I suspect cared less.

With such a fine record as Aldeburgh has in the sea-affair there should be someone still there who can put his finger on the various old nameboards, and tell us something about them.

A hundred years ago Chas. Dibdin shewed his interest in my subject by composing a song called " The Lookout," which would have applied equally well to Aldeburgh, Southwold, or Lowestoft Lookouts ; it is supposed to be sung by an old Gravesend pilot, of whom he says :

" Now cocking the spy-glass, and clearing the Nore,
    Why, Jack, there they come without end ;
    There's the *Neptune*, the *Glory*, and further in
        shore,
    Fame and *Liberty* making Gravesend.

" There's the homeward bound fleet from the
        Downs, only see ;
    So stored their topgallant masts bend ;
    There's the *Silkworm*, the *Beaver*, the *Ant* and the
        Bee,
    And all standing in for Gravesend.

" There's the *Fortitude* yonder, at danger that
        mocks ;
    The *Nimble* that swims like a tench ;
    The bold *Resolution*, that steers clear of rocks,
    The *Britannia* that laughs at the French."

These old wooden ship nameboards remind old
timers of the days when the Suffolk seaboard was
a kaleidescope of ever changing maritime views,
and when the adventures and trials of the crowd
of coasters, for ever on the move, were a source of
constant interest, and sometimes profit, to those
who watched from the shore.

Will those into whose hands these old relics
may come, see that they get a coat of tar and paint
once in a while ; they have weathered many a gale,
both at sea and ashore, and many of them are good
for years, with a little care.

XIV

A SUFFOLK SONNET

THIS appeared anonymously in the *Eastern Daily Press* about ten years ago and I believe the author is still unknown.

It is much too good to be lost and I have therefore obtained permission from the editor to include it here with my best respects to the author ; a real Suffolk man I am satisfied :

In my ow'd pightle where the Dickey feed,
The mavishes and fulfers fare to git
Allus enow to eat—That fare to fit
Wholly what our owd Raverend say and read;
How ba-ads and gillyflowers git what they need,
But when he say as how that there was writ
About *me* tew, thass suffin past my wit.

Twelve shillins is my wage, that is indeed,
And my owd Mawther, she say, partner bor,
" Thass them there childen they haint got no
    shues,
There aint no money for no Sunday jint,
You can't afford no bare, nor northin " Lor
Thass no good mobbin—That was writ for Jews,
I'm orf to the owd Hoss Shues for a pint.

XV

WITCHCRAFT IN SUFFOLK

THIS deep-rooted, popular superstition dates back to very early days, to the time of the Chaldeans, of the famous witch of Endor, of whom you can read in the twenty-eighth chapter of Samuel I. (my great-great-grandfather's Bible gives a picture of Saul and the witch calling up Samuel ;) Jezebel, whose witchcrafts are so many ; the Law of Moses, which lays it down that a witch should not be allowed to live (Ex. 22-18), and the twelve tables of Roman Law also providing against the black art, the punishment even then being burning. The Norsemen, of course, were steeped in witchcraft, and the Finns were the greatest masters of it, a tradition which exists to this day on board ship. The Vikings divided the art into two classes— Galdr, which was high-class sorcery used by wizards for noble purposes, and Seid, used mostly for evil ends, and principally by women. Apropos of this, the authors of " Hexenhammer," the fifteenth century German book of witchcraft, unkindly say that the art is more natural to women than to men, on account of the inherent wickedness of their hearts. It is possible the Vikings introduced the craft into England, where it was looked upon as paganism, and, by the laws of Ethelred, witches were to be banished. It may be that the Norse blood in the Suffolk people made them most tenacious and credulous supporters of this superstition, and there can be little doubt that our forefathers were desperately scared of being " overlooked " by witches. The rules to avoid such a calamity were endless, and many still survive. According to Ipswich Petty Plea Rolls, 27 and 28 Ed. I., Joan Haltebe recovered damages from Jn. Gyn, master of the ship *La Garlande*, Jn. le Sailyeur, Stace baker of Oreford and others for calling her sorcerer and pympledehore.

In King Henry VI., Shakespeare brings in Margery Jourdain, or Jourdemayne, the " cunning witch of Eye " (in Suffolk), and makes her raise a spirit in a magic circle to foretell the fate of the King and of the Dukes of Suffolk and Somerset. Bolingbroke is made to say " Mother Jourdain, be you prostrate and grovel on the earth and let us to our work." Suffolk books do not say much of this celebrated lady, but elsewhere it is on record that in 1432 she was imprisoned in Windsor Castle, with others, on a charge of sorcery, and was discharged on finding security for good behaviour. This was just a year after Joan of Arc had been sentenced by a French bishop and burnt, nominally for the same offence, but actually for having beaten us. Apparently Margery was unregenerate, for we find that in 1442-3 the Duchess of Gloucester was accused of treason by sorcery, and as " ayder and

counsailer to the sayde duchess," Margery Jour-
dayne, surnamed the witch of Eye, was charged
with devising a waxen image of the King, intending
to waste and destroy him, and, being convicted,
Margery was duly burnt at Smithfield. Evidently,
it was upon this record that Shakespeare based his
scene, and one may add that the Duchess did
public penance for her share, and that her husband,
good Duke Humphrey, was in due course murdered
at Bury in 1446, when Henry VI.'s Parliament
assembled there. It is said that De la Pole, Duke
of Suffolk, arranged this business for the Queen,
Margaret of Anjou. Incidentally, the Bury folk
put the Duke into such good Suffolk pickle that,
centuries later, when he was unearthed at St.
Albans Cathedral, he was found to be in quite
good condition. The whole story is related at
length in the second part of King Henry VI.

All the same, it does not appear that witchcraft
was a statutory crime until it was included in an
Act of 1541, which, having been repealed by
Edward VI., was re-enacted by 5 Elizabeth, c. 16.
This Act set out the various grades of witchcraft,
and made them felony, and it was followed by an
Act of James I., declaring witchcraft, sorcery,
charm or enchantment, felony without benefit of
clergy ; that is, persons able to read and write
could not claim exemption, as they could from
certain crimes. These Acts have all been long since
repealed, and the only surviving relic of those
times is to be found in the part of the Vagrants

Act dealing with fortune-tellers, still a popular entertainment.

It was not until the seventeenth century that people got busy smelling out and persecuting witches, leading to that unpleasant chapter in Suffolk history which tells of Matthew Hopkins, Witchfinder-General, who owed his office to the fanaticism of the Puritans, and was commissioned by Parliament in 1644-5-6 to travel the Eastern Counties to discover witches. According to some accounts, this repulsive tormentor of poor old country people was son of Jas. Hopkins, minister of Wenham, Suffolk, but moved to Manningtree, in Essex, while other authorities state that he was a native of Manningtree. In 1644 he secured the conviction of forty people at Bury, who were hanged on the Thinghow, just outside the town. In 1645 he visited Ipswich, and procured the conviction of Old Mother Lakeland for having sold herself to the devil, and for having inter alia wrought the destruction of Henry Reade and his ship and John Beale and his ship. She was burnt at Ipswich on the 9th September, 1645, but, the day before, the witchfinder set out for Aldeburgh, where he was so successful that seven poor wretches were hung, at a cost to the town of £10 7s., of which Matthew received £6; while the hangman only got 7s. He appears to have exacted a fee of 20s. for every parish visited, whether he did any business or no.

Hopkins' principal methods were either to strip

the victim and search for the concealed teats at
which the devil's imps were suckled, and any
likely marks were probed with three-inch pins,
or to swim her in a convenient pool, having first
tied thumbs and toes together crossways. Some
accounts say the victim was wrapped in a sheet,
but the picture of ducking a witch in my Defoe's
" History of the Devil " shows her being splounced
in, broom and all, with arms and legs free, while a
small urchin dances for joy and waves his hat on
the bank. A witch pit still exists at the back of
The Grove, Woodbridge, but has just been half
destroyed by that appalling byepass road now in
course of construction. "The Norfolk Garland"
states that a deep pool in the Waveney, near
Harleston, is still known as the " Witches' Pool,"
and I fear that many of our Suffolk ponds have
similar associations. If the person floated, it was
a sign of guilt, while those who sank were acquitted,
but had a good chance of being drowned. One
other method, known as " waking a witch," was in
use, and consisted in tricing the suspected person
up, and keeping her or him awake, day and night,
until a confession was forthcoming. It is said that
Hopkins also caused sixteen witches to be hung
at Yarmouth, others at Stowmarket, and many
more in Suffolk and Essex. The Crosby Records
say two hundred were indicted during the years
1644-6, and about half of them executed. But when
this crusade began to pall, it was proposed at one
of the Suffolk villages he visited that the Witch-

finder himself should be " swum," and as he, like
so many others, floated, he was hanged out of
hand in 1647-8, but not until he had published
in 1647 " The Discovery of Witches," in which
he takes as his text Exodus xxii. 18, " Thou shalt
not suffer a witch to live." The original can be
seen in the British Museum and has a curious
frontispiece.

Says Ralpho, in Part II. of " Hudibras,"

" Has not this present Parliament
A Ledger to the Devil sent ?
Fully impower'd to treat about
Finding revolted witches out ?
And has not he, within a year
Hang'd three-score of 'em in one shire ?
Some only for not being drowned,
And some for sitting above ground,
Whole days and nights, upon their breeches,
And, feeling pain, were hanged for witches.
Who after proved himself a witch,
And made a rod for his own breech."

Ledger is apparently an obscure reference to
Hopkins.

Still, the persecution lingered on, and anyone
having a grudge against a neighbour could accuse
her of being a witch. In 1649 Ann Camell was
indicted at Southwold for felony and witchcraft,
but the case was taken to Westminster, on the
ground that the indictment only said the prisoner

" practicavit diabolicas artes," and did not specify
the acts. Prisoner pleaded not guilty and that she
had been twice acquitted upon other similar
malicious charges. She was admitted to bail, the
case to be heard at the next Suffolk Assizes ;
unfortunately the result is not known. Incidentally
in 1603 a Thomas Camell was bailiff at Southwold,
and in old documents a part of Victoria Street,
Southwold, is called " Camell's Lane," and the
church register records the names of many Camells.
Her husband, Thomas, and Zachary Baggs, a
" sufficient Citizen and Fishmonger of London,"
were her sureties. One may assume from this that
Camell was interested in the fishing industry and
was a person of some standing, but, like poor
old John Lewis, for fifty years parson of Brandeston,
Suffolk, who was " swum " in the Castle ditch
at Framlingham, this did not save his wife from
persecution.

In 1648 John Sterne, of Lawshall, Suffolk, wrote :
" A Confirmation and Discovery of Witchcraft,
containing these several particulars ; that there
are Witches called bad Witches and Witches
untruely called good or white Witches, and what
manner of people they be and how they may be
known &c.," from which one gathers that he was
a disciple of the Witchfinder-General, and, indeed,
the campaign against witches lasted many years
after Hopkins met the punishment which fitted
his crime, for in 1644 occurred the well-known
prosecution of Rose Cullender and Amy Duny of

Lowestoft for bewitching two children. At their trial at Bury the otherwise enlightened Sir Thomas Browne, of Norwich, was called and expressed his opinion that the two Pacey girls were really bewitched and that in Denmark there had lately been a great discovery of witches. This evidence, from such a source, seems to have decided Sir Matthew Hale to leave it to the jury, and the two poor creatures were condemned and hanged. A popular account of this trial was published in London in 1682 by W. Shrewsbury. In 1694 Mother Mummings, of Hartest, was tried at Bury Assizes but acquitted, but in the previous year the Rev. Samuel Potts, of Sudbury, published " A faithful narrative of the wonderful and extraordinary fits which Mr. Thomas Spatchett (late of Dunwich and Cookley) was under by witchcraft." The last conviction for witchcraft was in 1712, but the prisoner was not executed ; it seems, however, that the practice of swimming people for witches was continued for many years more.

The following letter about a Suffolk man witch is from a MS. inserted in my copy of the " Suffolk Garland " and so far as I know has not been printed before. It appears to have been written to a Mr. John Morley.

" Halstead, August, 1732.

" Sir,

" The narrative which I gave you in relation to Witchcraft and which you have requested me to repeat is as follows :—

"There was one Mr. Collett, a smith by trade, of Haveningham in the County of Suffolk and formerly a servant in Sir John Duke's family, in Benhall near Saxmundham, Suffolk, who (as it was customary with him) assisted the dairy maid to churn or to make butter and not being able (as the phrase is) 'to make the butter come' he threw an hot iron into the churn under a notion that there was Witchcraft in the case. At that time a man, who was employed as Labourer and then at work in carrying off dung in the yard, cryed out in a terrible manner 'They have killed me' still keeping his hand upon his back intimating where the pain was and died upon the spot. The poor man's cloaths were taken off and the servants found to their surprise, the mark of the iron that was heated and thrown into the churn deeply imprinted upon his back. This account I had from Mr. Collett's own mouth, who, being a man of unblemished character I verily believe to be a matter of fact.

"I am, Sir,
"Yr. obliged servant,
"Sam Manning."

In 1795, according to the *Ipswich Journal*, a Mrs. Greygoose was "swum" in a pond near Stanning-field Church, Suffolk, it being alleged that she had six imps named Silcock, Wisky, Turntail, Toby, Tarran and Tegg. The *Suffolk Chronicle* recorded that in July, 1825, Isaac Stebbings was "swum" at Wickham Skeith Green, Suffolk, for a wizard, in the presence of the village constable and hundreds of people. Stebbings appears to have swum like a cork, but in neither of these cases is it noted what transpired after the proof, except that the clergyman and churchwardens, to their credit, interfered and prevented any further test of Isaac. Eye seems to have been a good district for witches, and in the latter part of the eighteenth century it boasted another practitioner of wide repute, in Old Nan Barret, who was consulted by people over a radius of thirty or forty miles, and could punish any who did not pay her fees promptly. Old Mother Maddie, of Yarmouth, is said to have been the last wise woman of any standing on the East Coast, but I well remember, many years ago, being taken to see a reputed witch in my native Suffolk village ; she was a very dirty, ugly, old person, and sat by the fire smoking a clay pipe and mumbling to herself, while her cat occupied a chair on the opposite side of the hearth. When Christmas Eve came round, the dare-devils of the village placed a nice log of wood on her doorstep after dark, which the poor old soul joyfully put on the fire next day, but the scamps had bored the log, put in a charge of gunpowder, and plugged it, so that in due course it went off like a gun, and old woman, cat and fire were blown all ways about the room.

I cannot help thinking that many of these old women were rather proud of being thought witches, and that the distinction often secured them consideration and actual benefits, most people wishing to stand well with them, or fearing to cross such dangerous neighbours, so that in a way they may be said to have asked for their troubles. To conclude, I will borrow from " Suffolk Folklore," to which and to Mr. V. B. Redstone, I wish to make acknowledgments, an amusing story of a Suffolk labourer, who, hearing of a wise woman's charm for hurting an enemy, had it repeated until he was quite sure of the formula, and then said : " S'elp me lucky ! I'll try that on my brother, that I wool."

XVI

ALL IN THE DAY'S WORK OF A SUFFOLK
FISHERMAN

NEARLY thirty years ago Mr. Walter Wood wrote
some stories of the men of the North Sea, chiefly
of Yorkshire stock; we heard of many, many
brave actions by Trawler Reserve crews from all
parts, during the War, but I wish to draw attention
to a more recent epic of the North Sea, in which
figured prominently a young Southwold skipper,
son of a very old fisherman friend of my own.

It is not my intention, nor is it necessary, to
dress it up in any fancy language, but to give
the chief performer's own bare narrative, as set
down for the information of the Board of Trade,
given me by one of his owners.

I would only just like to dwell upon the facts
that the service lasted from Sunday evening to
Wednesday night, by daylight and dark, in a
December gale, which would mean such conditions
as can only be properly appreciated by those who
have faced such weather in small craft, upon,
what Mr. Wood has called, in the book referred
to, " the restless and ruthless North Sea."

S.T. *Elector*, L.T. 579 AND SMACK *Peaceful* L.T. 99
STATEMENT BY THE MASTER OF THE S.T. *Elector*.

When dodging to windward on Sunday, December 8th, 1929, about sixty-five miles E.N.E. from Smiths Knoll Light Vessel at about 6 p.m., the watch reported there were red rockets and flares going up into the S.E. of us. We rang on speed at once and proceeded in that direction and came across a smack with its foremast gone riding head to sea with a sea anchor out. Owing to such a heavy sea running and the wind blowing a gale force, we went as close under her lee as the circumstances would permit, and in the glare of the flares we could see the crew of the smack lined at the rail shouting. We caught " alright " and something about daylight so we came to the conclusion that the crew were in no immediate danger. We kept a good lookout on her and stood by her till daylight, which proved no easy matter as we had such heavy squalls of rain, and at times we could not see him at all. At daylight we proceeded up to him as close as we could. Not being able to get any lines to him by throwing, he floated his cod line to leeward on his lifebuoys and fish trunks and we dodged up and picked them up.

We then bent on a larger rope with which he heaved our two warps on board with his capstan and shackled them into his trawl warp, and we commenced to tow him. Owing to so much heavy seas running we dare not try to tow him only dead slow. We had not been towing him more than one hour, when his trawl warp parted and we had to go round and pick him up again. This time he shackied our warps into his chain cable, and we started to tow him again.

All went well until about 3 p.m. (Monday), when we parted one of our warps so we had to heave back on the other warp and shackled on two new wire bridles that we had down below. We started to tow again, and at about 6.30 p.m. we parted from him again and when we hove in our wires we found that his chain cable had parted.

When we found him again he was riding with his sea anchor out again and as the weather had not improved we decided to stand by till daylight (Tuesday). During the night we got two lengths of our heavy cable up and shackled our broken warp to the other end, and at daylight we got connection with him again. After he got our broken wire on to his capstan we threw our cable overboard and slacked our bridles away until he got our cable on board, and then we started to tow him again. We were towing him slowly until about 3 p.m. when we saw the crew making frantic signs for us to stop towing. We hove back until we could hear the skipper of the smack shout and tell us that we would have to stop towing as his capstan and tow post had pulled out, ripping her decks up and her stem was coming out as well. She looked waterlogged and did not look like lasting half the night afloat.

We decided that if we could manage to get the crew off before dark that was their only chance. He was flush with the water and our bows were so much higher. I decided to give him our quarter which we succeeded in doing, and the three scrambled up and were pulled on board over our stern as soon as we touched him. After that we stowed up our trawls, which had washed and broken adrift, and got our chains and broken wires down below.

We missed the lights the crew left on the smack, and came to the conclusion she had foundered. So we shaped our course for Lowestoft, arriving at about 9 p.m. Wednesday, December 11th.

(Signed) W. H. Winter,
Skipper of S.T. *Elector*.

I am glad to be able to add that the Board of Trade awarded a silver cup to Captain Winter, in recognition of the seamanship displayed on this occasion, and that he and his crew also had watches presented to them for this same rescue.

XVII

CHILDISH THINGS

"Old Customs ; Oh I love the sound,
However simple they may be ;
What e'er with time hath sanction found,
Is welcome and is dear to me."
(CLARE, THE PEASANT POET).

THOSE who have become supermen, and utterly
put away childish things, had better skip this
chapter, but I believe there are many who will
find something of interest in it.

Imprimis, there have survived to me three items
of my mother's repertoire which I suspect are
traditional, and may go back some way ; through
a pretty varied, and wide range of reading and
research, I have kept a look out for any references
bearing upon the subjects, but never a word, nor
a hint, have I found ; it may be that some reader
will be able to help.

Sir Nicholas Wood always suggests to my mind
a dour, surly old Roundhead, twice the age of the
plaintive lady, who for some inexplicable reason
appears anxious to wed him, and to have a little
life at the wedding.

Our mother would give the lady's part in a high soprano, and Sir Nicholas in the gruffest, grumpiest tone he could assume, about an octave lower, but perhaps in the original it was a dialogue ; the tune wasn't much.

To the best of my recollection it ran thus :

Lady : When shall we be married ? my dear Sir Nicholas Wood.
Knight : We'll be married a' Monday provided the weather be good.

L : Can't we be married any sooner ? my dear Sir Nicholas Wood.
K : Why, would you be married a' Sunday ? I think you must be mad.

L : What shall we have for our dinner ? my dear Sir Nicholas Wood.
K : We'll ha' beans and bacon, and I think t'will be wondrous good.

L : Can't we have anything else ? my dear Sir Nicholas Wood.
K : Why, would you have mutton and capers ? I think you must be mad.

L : Who shall we have to our wedding ? my dear Sir Nicholas Wood.
K : We'll ha' your father and mother, and I think t'will be wondrous good.

L : Can't we have anyone else ? my dear Sir Nicholas Wood.

K : Why, would you have half the nation ? I know you must be mad.

The second is a fragment relating to the disposal of Cock Robin's corpse, after he had been done to death in some forgotten mode.

Who Roger Mahone was, and what he had to do with Cock Robin in a Suffolk Folk Tale I do not understand, nor is it clear what the sort of Greek Chorus were, who appear under the title " Everyone " and dutifully support Roger in his wildest flights.

It may have been some political skit, the application of which is now entirely lost, and may have nothing to do with Suffolk, but I tell what I remember of it in the hope that some light may be shed upon this queer nursery ditty. From the reference to " Gig-lamps " it is nothing like so old as Sir Nicholas ; I rather think we children came in as " Everyone " with the last line :

What shall we do with his body ?
Pies, Pies, said Roger Mahone,
Pies, Pies, said everyone.

What shall we do with his feathers ?
Beds, Beds, said Roger Mahone,
Beds, Beds, said everyone.

What shall we do with his eyes ?
Gig-lamps, Gig-lamps, said Roger Mahone,
Gig-lamps, Gig-lamps, said everyone.

What shall we do with his claws ?
Scratch-backs, Scratch-backs, said Roger Mahone,
Scratch-backs, Scratch-backs, said everyone.

The last verse was the climax, and it was empha-
sized by pretended violent scratching of the backs
of the juvenile audience, and generally led to a
merry scramble with much laughter.

The third, and last, is a queer tongue-twister,
which I cannot explain in any way. The object is
to say it all in a single breath, and this most will
find a bit of an effort :

Theophilus Thwaite Thwabbit thrust his hand
    through 333 thick and thin thistles
Did Theophilus Thwaite Thwabbit thrust his hand
    through 333 thick and thin thistles
If Theophilus Thwaite Thwabbit thrust his hand
    through 333 thick and thin thistles
Where are the 333 thick and thin thistles Theo-
    philus Thwaite Thwabbit thrust his hand
    through ?

It may be only a home made variant of the
industrious Peter Piper, but was often trotted out
for the edification, or discomfiture of small
visitors.

There is a village in Suffolk called Thwaite, or Twaite I believe by the natives, and two in Norfolk, but I do not know if this old jingle has anything to do with any of them; the name is said to derive from the Norse "thweit," a woodland clearing, and is common in the north.

Mr. Thwabbit must have been, as the boy said, some "fabulous monster now extinct."

If a threatening thunderstorm was heralded by a rainbow when we were out for a walk, a wetting could be avoided by hurrying home at top speed, repeating all the way the following distich:

Rainbow; Rainbow; tickle a stone,
Don't let it rain till I get home.

I wonder if in the harvest fields boys still cut " squakers " from the stiff new-cut wheat straw; we used to cut off a length with a knot at one end, and then slice a slip back to the knot to form the reed. This when properly cut, and put well inside the mouth, would produce a horrible, strident note, which could be varied according to the length of the reed.

If it would not sound at first the ritual was to roll it between the palms of the hands, and recite as follows:

Rake ye; Rake ye,
If ye don't squake
I'll break ye.

The crow-keeping boy's cry was :

> Car-whoo ; Car-whoo ;
> Hare come the clappers
> To knock ye down backards,
> Car-who-o-o.

Another version in use in Woodbridge district was :

> Car-whoo ; Car-whoo ; yow owd black crow.
> Goo fly awa to Sutton,
> If yow stop heer t'll cost ye dear,
> I'll kill ye dead as mutton.

A choice ditty was the warning against the gipsies, and was given very staccato with an emphasis on each final word :

> My Mother *said*,
> I never *should*,
> Play with the Gipsies
> In the *wood*.

> My Mother *said*,
> If I *did*,
> She'd clout my head
> With the *saucepan-lid*.

I was told in my youth that the following lines used to be painted on a new waggon in the olden

days, but I never saw them in my time ; the elision
in the last line is true Suffolk :

> Here I am, red, green, and blue,
> Ready for your work to do ;
> Keep me clean, and lend me not,
> For if you do you'll suffer fo't.

When sitting by the firelight in winter evenings
we would tap the jolly old logs with the poker,
and send sparks flying up the chimney ; the game
was to send single sparks at first, saying :

> There goes the parson,
> There goes his clerk,
> There go the little boys
> All up in the dark,

the last line being emphasised by a good stir up,
and a shower of sparks.

I suppose we do not use the same coal nowadays,
as one seldom sees one of those round, hollow,
cinders fly out of the fire, which as children we
used to call money boxes, and consider a sign of
luck, but quite otherwise if it was one of the long
shaped variety called coffins.

One of the catches to be said very quickly was :

" The black dog danced on the barn floor barefoot."

Another was :

" Three blue beads in a blue bladder,
Rattle blue beads, rattle blue bladder."

It is almost impossible to say either correctly at
any pace.

The one poor widow round game of my day
ran :

" An' now you're married we wish ye joy,
An' every year a gal or a boy,"

an achievement which would be sadly unpopular
nowadays.

Another round game which I have never seen
in print was this :

" Round and round the Vinegar shop,
The Vinegar shop, the Vinegar shop,
Round and round the Vinegar shop,
An' hare we goo with a bop ; bop ; BOP."

Bop is Suffolk for the bob curtsey which women
used to drop ; at each " bop " the performers
would bob, and with the last all would plump
down on the ground.

I remember us all picking lint for the wounded
in the Franco-Prussian War ; old linen was cut
into long strips, and we then picked out the weft
with needles ; also the discussions in the kitchen
about the Prewshins and the Rewshins, who were
supposed to be in it somewhere.

Later on when at school at Yarmouth I recollect the Reserves being called out in 1878, when the "Rewshins" were, as usual, said to be preparing for War; the men wore dark blue uniforms, and shakos with cocks' feather plumes, like I used to wear in the London Rifle Brigade forty years ago. I saw a battalion of them paraded on the North Drive, in front of their Colonel's house, for Church Parade.

The Prince of Wales used to come to Yarmouth then every year to inspect the Norfolk Artillery Militia, of which he was Colonel. In 1872 he opened the then new Grammar School as well, and we generally used to wangle a holiday out of him to see the regiment inspected on the South Denes. It was an awful blunder disbanding the Artillery Militia, as was realized when the War started; I also saw them firing the old sixty-four pounder M.L. guns in the South Battery, and remember that if you stood exactly behind the gun you could see the ball travelling. Yarmouth Roads were then a panorama of shipping of all nations, and how the east wind stung you upon the Drive: After the 18th January, 1881, the "Janiwary Gale," I saw seven vessels ashore on Yarmouth Beach when I went back to school. Going through our old Head's papers, at the Ipswich Free Library recently (Canon J. J. Raven, D.D., F.S.A.), I was honoured to find that he had kept the letters I wrote him in after life.

One quaint old Dickens character comes back

to me as I write of the days of my youth ; I am
not sure if she was Norfolk, or Suffolk, but she
rejoiced in the resonant, alliterative name of
Hannah Hoggett, and was servant to my grandmother in early days ; she then married, but after
being left a widow would always come back to
any of the family when wanted.

She had an everlasting tongue (which my
mother said was hung in the middle and wagged
both ends), and the Tony Weller fashion of turning
Vs into Ws and vice-versa ; her conversation
would run thus :

" Vell, Vell, Miss, now vot do you think ? I
got my taters on this morning, and ven I made up
the fire I set them a one side out of the smoke ;
by'm bye the Missis she come in the kitchen, and
vot do you think she done ? poor old dear, took
the saucepan and lumped it down in the middle of
the fire and ven I vent back there was my taters
as black as sut ; so I says, ' Vell there Maam, now
you ha' wexed me, jest look at my taters, enough
to choke a black), and vot do you think she say,
as cule as a cowcumber, ' Vy,' says she, ' Hannah
Hoggett,' says she, vich my name is Dobbs now,
D,o,b,b,s, not D,o,double b,s, like some people
spell it, ' vot matter,' says she, ' vy vash 'em,'
says she, ' pump on 'em.' Oh I vos wexed, and
my taters wholly spylt ; and look there now, if
that there gal Ann hain't left that there candle in
the pantry agin. Vell, Vell, I niver did see such a

gal ; Ann, you'a left that there candle agin ;
ANN, vy vere have you got to ? "

A good faithful old soul, of the days when maids
were friends for life.

Suffolk people frequently use W for V, as
" woilet," for violet, and " wassel," for vessel,
but I do not think the converse holds good here,
although I believe Norfolkers turn V into W
sometimes.

XVIII

RECORDS OF GREAT FIRES IN SUFFOLK

IT is probable that the dearth in East Suffolk of those beautiful half-timbered houses, so many of which are to be seen in Mid. and West Suffolk, is accounted for by the devastating fires which took place frequently in the eastern half of the county in the sixteenth to the eighteenth centuries, and which perhaps were rendered so destructive by the high winds from the sea, to which that district was, and still is, particularly liable.

The Victoria County History states that hardly a town in Suffolk appears to have escaped a disastrous fire, and that on the coast, fire was but too apt to follow in the wake of tempest.

I have collected these notes of some of the outstanding conflagrations from 1539 to 1749:

1539.—Copinger states that a fire occurred in Beccles that year but gives no details.

1583.—Gardner relates that Walberswick was a great sufferer from fire before that date, details also wanting.

1586. November 29.—Beccles half destroyed through a chimney catching fire during a high wind ; a calamity which was celebrated by one Thomas Delone in, " A proper newe sonet declaring the lamentation of Beckles Suffolke, which was in the great winde upon St. Andrewes eve last past most pitifully burned with fire, to the loss by estimation of twentie thousande pound and upwarde and to the number of foure score dwelling houses." This sonnet is in black letter, and was discovered in the binding of an old book in the Royal Society's Library; I cull a couple of verses as a sample:

" But now beholde my great decay,
　　Which on a sodaine came;
My sumptuous buildings burned be
　　By force of fires flame;
A careless wretch, most rude in life,
　　His chymney set on fire,
The instrument, I must confesse,
　　Of God's most heavie ire.

The flame whereof increasing still
　　The blustering windes did blowe,
And into divers buildings by
　　Disperst it to and fro;
So, kindling in most grievous sort,
　　It waxed huge and hie;
The river then was frozen, so
　　No water they could come by."

1596.—Southwold was pitifully defaced by fire on a Friday.

1606.—The Vicarage House at Lowestoft burnt down, the Parish Register, and many of the ancient Town Records destroyed.

1631. 10th June.—Forty houses burned at Walberswick and eight more on the 3rd July; the diary of John Rous (Camden Society) relates "Two women and a boy of sixteen executed at Bury, on the 18th July, for burning Walberswick. The boy upon his death, affirmed that his sister councelled and the other woman gave him fire."

1633.—Walberswick Town, or a great part thereof burnt. Gardner records that in this case also the prisoners were sent to Bury for trial, and it seems just possible that these two notes refer to the same fire.

1644. March 10.—One hundred and forty houses burnt at Lowestoft, £10,000 damage; the fishing community suffered very severely.

1652.—Great fire at Bungay, "A sadd and lamentable tyme."

1654.—Ipswich, "great damage having lately befallen to the town by fire, it is ordered that all straw-kilns in this town shall be suppressed."

1659. April 25.—Great fire at Southwold. Two hundred and thirty-eight houses and all public buildings burnt, three fourths of the town burnt. damage £40,000; Yarmouth sent twenty combs of wheat, ten of rye, and £10 in cash to relieve the distress; it is said the town never recovered from that fire, three hundred families were ruined, and many left the place never to return.

1662.—Beccles once more damaged by fire, and again in 1667 and 1669.

1670. August 14.—Midnight, the wind being very high there happened a sudden, dreadful, and lamentable fire in Lowestoft, for which a collection was made.

1676.—A destructive fire at Blythburgh; loss £1,800.

1683.—Walberswick again set on fire, "Paid Watchmen for watching the Fire in Town 1s. 6d." (Gardner).

1678.—Beccles received £22 11s. 5d. from Yarmouth towards relief of the poor sufferers by the late fire; no other record found.

1688. March 1.—Nearly all Bungay destroyed by fire, one church and one hundred and ninety houses, the loss put at £30,000.

1703.—Walberswick ruined by fire.

1717. November 12.—Another terrible fire at Lowestoft, the wind pretty fresh at south-east, damage £1,000.

1744.—Debenham suffered severely from fire.

1749. April 14.—One third of the remains of Walberswick were destroyed by fire, from a chimney catching fire in a hard wind at west.

It must be remembered there were no fire brigades in those days, and that many of the houses were timber framed or built, and thatched, and when a fire once got good hold the only means of checking it was by pulling houses down in its path.

A very scarce old broadsheet entitled "The Woefull and Lamentable wast and spoile done by a suddaine Fire in S. Edmonds-Bury in Suffolke, on Munday the tenth of Aprill 1608," has a crude woodcut of the fire in progress ; the roofs of several houses are in flames, upon which three men are pouring water from buckets carried up a ladder, while others are pulling down a gable end by means of a fire-crome, with ropes attached, and that was the best that one of our largest towns could do in 1608.

In 1594 Thetford, Norfolk, ordered, " that every burgesse provide twoo bucketts, and everye comoner one buckett, and everye other house-holder a maukyn for the quenching of fyre when casualtie shall happen within the towne." (A Maulkin was a pole with a kind of mop head to hold water for beating out the fire.) In the Tower of Haughley Church are, or were, a number of leather fire buckets bearing dates in the eighteenth century.

I have a vivid recollection of a night of panic in Halesworth some thirty-five years back, when but for the fire brigades, half the old property in that town would have gone up in flames.

Again, there was no Fire Insurance until 1681, when the first Fire Office was established, " at the backside of the Royal Exchange ; " the Norwich Union was not founded until 1797, for the Eastern Counties, and almost the only relief the sufferers obtained was by means of briefs, by which national, or local, collections were authorized to be made in the churches.

In respect of the 1659 fire Southwold was granted a brief, dated 11th June, 1659, addressed to all Parsons, Justices, Headboroughs etc., throughout England, a copy is set out in Gardner's History, and in very many churchwardens' books will be found accounts of the collection in aid ; the entry at Harleston cum Redenhall is as follows, " 1659, 17th of August. Recd. of Mr. John Hubberd, and Mr. Fenn the breife for Southwold wth fifteene pounds eleaven shillings fyve pence halfe pennye, and two od pieces of monye to the value of foure pence collected in Harleston cu Reddenhall and Wortwell for the re-building of the said towne."

In Old Newton Register this brief is thus recorded, " Collected in Old Newton for a barning in Sold in Suff. 10,000 pounds loss in July 1659 collected the sume of fower pounds seventine shillings. . . . £4 17s. od."

Bungay was granted a brief for the 1688 fire ; Earsham gave £46.

Cratfield Papers contain the following, " 1633. Laid out to Walberswick brief the 20th January for a burning the loss £3,801 15s. 2d. . . . 17s. 6d."

These statutory briefs, called " Kings Briefs " were issued out of Chancery, and consequently, it may be affirmed, were not obtained without considerable expense : indeed it is said that very often the charges swallowed up half the amount collected. An entry in the Dunwich Chamberlains' account shews the mode of circulating a brief :

" 1619. Feb. 13.—The King's Protection for collecting money for the haven being obtained, and briefs from the Council, and letters, it is agreed that Mr. John Back shall travel along with the Judges going the Lent Assizes circuits, and lay the briefs and do what is fitting for the good of the town." The amount so collected in London was £33 3s. 9d., and the expenses were £17 3s. 6d.

Contributions in aid of Beccles were raised in Norfolk, and Suffolk, and in the Norwich Mayor's Court Book is the following, " William Fleming, preacher of Beccles raised in Court of Mr. Mayor £30 10s. 8d., which was collected in this city towards the re-edifying of Beccles Church which was lately burnt."

" And thus I ende my wofull song,
    Beseeching God I may
Remaine a mirrour to all such,
    That doe in pleasure stay ;
And that amongst their greatest mirth
    And chiefest ioye of all,
They yet may have a heart to thinke
    Of Beckles sodaine fall."

XIX

BYGONE WALBERSWICK

Punch celebrated Walberswick by a Lay entitled " Artist on the Brain," which I believe was a product of the late Saville Clarke's prolific " cerebrum," in which he said :

" I always did love Walberswick, and have in
    olden time,
Immortalized its lonely shores, in sentimental
    rhyme,"

and thus referred to my old friend the Ferryman there :

" They sketch the Ferryman's old hut, the reeds
    that sway and nod,
The Early Christian countenance of Charon,
    Mister Todd."

I am afraid that very few will remember old Geo. Todd, the ferryman between Walberswick and Southwold, of fifty years ago. He told me he only took the job on for another man for a few days, but the man never came back, and Todd had then been crossing the water for forty odd years.

He was a most picturesque character, beloved of the artists of those days, and appears in many pictures of the ferry of that period. (" A Ferry on the Blyth " by Grace, No. 839 Royal Academy 1877 ; Walberswick Ferry, Macallum, and Walberswick Ferry by Evershed.) He was also latterly, like most old folk, somewhat short and surly, at times.

On one occasion he appeared in a brand-new pair of highlows, a great event in people's lives when boots were made to last, and were kept well oiled ; a cheerful soul, who was crossing, remarked, " Why Mr. Todd you've got a new pair of boots on to-day." " I know," replied Charon, " I put 'em there."

Todd used to lay the boat cunningly on the tide, and let the stream set her across with the minimum of exertion ; one day I was crossing, and as it was very wet, and blowing hard, I stood up to avoid the wet seats. Seeing how slow our progress was, I ventured to remark we were a long time getting over and Todd replied, " Yes, and if you don't set down it'll be a hell of a time."

The old man refused to attend the Jubilee Dinner, being then about eighty, on the ground that " he never had been to no Jubilee Dinners and he worn't a goin to begin at his time o' life."

Old Todd's son Harry, was a real deep water sailor man, and was at sea in the tea clippers and wool ships for years; at one time he served in the *Belted Will*, one of the famous fleet of tea ships of the 'sixties, of which Miss Fox-Smith wrote :

" By the old Pagoda Anchorage they lay full
    fifteen strong,
  And their spars were like a forest, and their
    names were like a song.
        Fiery Cross and *Falcon* there
        Lay with *Spindrift* doomed and fair,
  And Sir Lancelot of a hundred famous fights
    with wind and wave,
        Belted Will and *Hallowe'en*
        With *Leander* there were seen,
  And *Ariel* and *Titania* and *Robin Hood* the brave."

Harry told me once that as a young man he was away at sea for twelve years straight off, and never once wrote home; then one voyage he paid off somewhere down in the north and took the train to Lowestoft; on arrival he walked to Southwold, getting to the river about midnight. He found a boat on the bank, and paddled her across to Walberswick with the bottom boards, then went up to the old familiar cottage and knocked at the door.

He heard the old man lump out of bed, and come downstairs to the door and call out, " Whew's there," before he would open. His son replied,

" Thass Harry," and the old chap answered back quick, " That I know tain't," but then he heard his mother call out from the bed upstairs, " Why let him in father, thass the boy Harry." The door was cautiously opened, and so the sailor son came home from sea.

Harry Todd used to sing a song I well remember; I think he called it " Far, Far away," but Capt. Whall, in his collection of sea-songs calls it " Unmooring " and says it was a prime favourite with the real old shellback.

It begins :

" All hands on board, the Bosun cries,
    His voice like thunder roaring ;
All hands on board, his mates reply,
    'Tis the signal for unmooring.
Then your messenger bring to
Heave your anchor to the bow,
        And we'll think on those girls
        When we're far, far away,
        And we'll think on those girls
        When we're far, far away."

Walberswick has even been noticed in the aristocratic columns of the Court Circular, which set out the following notice copied from the Walberswick Chapel door :

" Nottice that atown
meeting Will be held
in the schoolroom on
Thursday 31 Dec. 1885
at seven oclock
to transeact som
parrish besness
hopping all will
atend that have enny
intrest in the parrish
    „   „ fen reeve "

" A ' Walserwig ' whisper heard over to Sowl,"
has become a Suffolk proverb (see Suffolk Folk
Lore, etc.).

As I am writing of Walberswick I may as well
give a few out of the way notes relating to the
shipping trade formerly carried on there, which
may be a help to someone who may undertake a
proper history of the place in olden days ; to
start with a small treatise could be written on the
correct way to spell its name ; the following gives
the champion effort I have found so far.

The Celys were great London wool merchants
in the fifteenth century, and in their Papers (Camden
Society) is the following note : " 4 Aug. 1478.
Mony I paid for frayght in the name of my fadyr
Rychard Cely as after aperythe be dyvars parcellz—
Item, the same day pd be me unto Robard Bell

master in the Andrew Whalldyrswhyke for an
sarplar vis viijd-premage jd."

I would explain that a sarplar of wool was a
pocket or half a sack.

20th of Henry viii.—A complaint was made from
" your poor widow Cristian Balard of Walbertus-
wyke, late wife of Richard Balard," alleging that
Robert owned a ship called the Christopher of
Walberswyke which had been wrongfully seized
at Sandwich, and detained whereby " the said
ship decayed, and lost all cables sails bitts and other
necessaries belonging to her," and that she had to
" hire another ship in the season for fishing for
the time of six weeks to her cost of £7 and because
the fishing was so far spent before she could get
another ship whereby she lost her fishing and by
reason whereof the master and mariners attempted
an action against your said plaintiff for the loss of
the fishing which was to the great hurt, harm,
damage, and hinderance of the said beseecher
above £40."

1485. *November* 10.—Richard Blitheburgh of
Walberswick left to " St. Andregh a mansor nette
of xii XX " (twelve score) also some interesting
bequests of nets of various sorts to other people—
Suffolk Wills, Archdeaconry Court.

1498. *October* 16.—The Will of Margaret Hoo
of Walberswick, so dated, and proved at Ipswich,
16th December, 1498, contains bequests to " John
Cryton, one manfare of depesenett " and " to

Isabell Chapell one depsenette " ; I take it that
" Mansor " and " manfare " are the same, and
refer to the number of nets each fisherman of the
crew would contribute towards the fleet ; this Will
is also interesting because it speaks of " Myn
tenement at ye Crosse." Is this the only mention
of a cross at Walberswick ?

The 12th of King Henry viii, Tuesday, January 8.—
A certain Nicholas Davyson of Walburswyk in
co. Suffolk mariner, placed himself recently in the
parish church of the town of Cley by the Sea in
co. Norfolk, and acknowledged that on the first
day of January the said year he broke into the
house of Robert Burford at Walburswyk, and
stole 13s. in a purse of the value of one half-
penny."

Nicholas had to abjure the kingdom, and the
Jury found that he possessed four law books which
went to the Lord of the Manor; no doubt the law
books put him up to claiming the ancient right
of sanctuary.

1513. *February* 16.—A commission was issued
to Thomas Beversham of Walberswick to man the
Thomas of Walberswick as a transport.

1545. *December* 11.—Acts of the Privy Council.

A letter to Richard Arnolde of " Warbaswicke "
Co. Suffolk, commanding him either to appear
forthwith personally before the " Lordes of the
Councell, orels before the Duke of Norfolk at his
howse at Kennynghall for not shewing his cockett
to the Commissioners for the Sea Costes in that

countrye and for his evill language used againste them."

1547. *November* 4.—Certificate of the sale of Walberswyk Church goods.

" The true certyficate of Roberd Carter, Wyllm Jaffery and John Vycarye Cherchewardens there—

" We certyfie that we w^t the cosent of the towne hathe sold iiij yers past a crosse ij peyer of chalys ij candelstykks a pax and a schepe—all these thynges ware sold at diu^{rse} tymes the prce of them xxxli."

1561.—Wm. Gaston of Walberswick, and Thos. Gray master of the James of Walberswick, 100 tons burden, complained to Mary, Queen of Scots that being in haven at Westmoney in Iceland they were cruelly underset, and invaded by some Scotchmen who spoiled them to the value of £2800.

1573. *November* 29.—Acts of Privy Council. Letter to the Commissioners for the Restrainte of Vittels in Suffolk thanking them for their pains " for the compounding of soche controversie as is betwixt the townes of Donwich Walversweek and Southould to signifie to eche of them that her Mties plesure is that eche of them send up hither sum discrete person of their towne sufficiently instructed to answer here."

1585.—The Admiralty Court Exemplifications (No. 23-211-13) shew that Walberswick shipping suffered losses by Spanish reprisals this year.

1587.—When England was preparing to receive the Armada the Commissioners reported " Walderswyck being a barred haven and which shifteth every easterly wynd ys therefore a place of no great dawnger."

1619.—From Walberswick to Yarmouth bailiffs re suppressing pirates.

"Our hartie Commendations unto you remembered we thinke that the Inhabitants of our towne of Walbersweek to be no memberse of yr port or are to be contributors with yow in anie such chardge; or that the Lordes of his Majesties privie Counsell do so intend it; for yow know that we have noe merchaunts at all dwelling in our towne or hath anie shipping within the same trading toward those Sothern partes. But onlie our cheifest trade is in fisher fare to the northern seas in small barkes fitting for the same purpose and yeldeth unto his Majestie yearlie out of the same Composition fishe; yet notwithstanding if it please the right honarable the lordes of his Majesties privie Counsell to think it meete that we being poor fishermen and our Inhabitants very poor for the most part to contribute towards the same chardge we shall be verie willing to our abilities to yealde unto anie reasonable chardge by our selves towards the same and soe we leave you to the protection of allmightie god from Walbersweeke this second day of Marche 1619.

Your loveing frindes to use
Henry Fraunces
N. Cripes
Thomas Cuxford."

1655.—Inhabitants of Southwold and Walberswick petition for enquiry into the state of their haven and means to amend it—it formerly set forth many ships but is now spoiled for want of piering.

It appears that Thomas Gardner, the Historian of Dunwich lived at Walberswick before he went to Southwold, or else chose to have his children baptized there; in the register will be found an entry on the 24th May, 1723, Redshaw Gardner, son of Thomas, and Rachel his wife, and on the 7th June 1724, Georg Redshaw Gardener, son of Thomas Gardener, and Rachel his Wife.

From the Diary of James Maggs, born at Walberswick, 12th February, 1797, died Southwold, 9th February, 1890, I cull these items:

1804. August 4.—Suffolk launched at Walberswick.

1827. February 24.—Harbour blocked, carriages to and fro. (This appears to have occurred frequently in those days.)

1883. October.—R. English's Clipper lost with all hands.

Of the Clipper's crew no less than seven were Walberswick men; the story of her loss was written by Capt. J. H. S. Benham, and it is an old, old story in the history of this little seafaring community; in 1814, the *Dunwich*, eighty-six tons, built at Walberswick, 1803, was lost with all hands, and every generation of Walberswick men has given its toll to the stern North Sea, and

there they have found " Rest, that shall hunger
no more, neither thirst any more, their eyes, and
mouths filled with the brown sea sand."

The name Maggs occurs at Leiston in 1674, and
the subject of this note was an auctioneer at Southwold, and the last coroner for the Boro, he erected
his tombstone, duly inscribed except for the date,
long years before his death; it used to be said
of him that he lived for over ninety years and
never saw the sun rise, but he left a most useful
little history of " The Port and Shipping of Southwold," and the Diary of local events from about
1816.

XX

A LA BONNE HEURE

A LIFEBOAT EPIC

OF my many lifeboat and longshore experiences
one will remain vividly in my memory until the
last, on account of its dramatic surroundings, and
successful issue, leading to full recognition by the
French Government. It happened this way:

We had a schoolboy relative to spend a week-end
in November, 1905, and the Sunday night of the
26-27th turned out very dirty, a strong gale of
wind at SSW all night turning off to WSW,
and moderating a bit at daybreak.

However we were up early to get breakfast in
time for the 7.30, and all started for the station;
just round the corner I met my sterling old friend,
Sam May, for over twenty years coxswain of our
lifeboats.

He was bustling along, and hailed me that he
was just coming for me as there was something
wrong on the Ness, and would I come at once to
the Coastguard Station, and see what I could
make of it.

We hurried round there, and perhaps it had got
a little lighter, or my sight was a bit quicker than

theirs that morning, for directly I turned the long glass on to Covehithe Ness I could see the masts of a sunken vessel, and a bunch of something at the masthead, which I took to be the crew.

"Why Sam," said I, "it's a ship sunk, and I can see the people hanging in the rigging; fire the gun quick, and let's be going."

So off we started pell-mell, and I called in at my house for a warmer jacket and oilskins, and had the happy thought to shove my camera into the pocket. I was then making my collection of lifeboat and wreck scenes, and this enabled me to score what journalists call "the scoop" of my life in that line.

The *Alfred Corry* lay on the Beach then, and the wind and sea, having gone down a bit, we were able to launch in record time at 7.30 a.m., and carry whole sails all the way; indeed when we saw a plume of smoke over the land towards Lowestoft, we guessed that a tug was on the way, and we pumped all the water ballast out, and crouched down to windward to try and beat the tug.

It was intensely exciting cracking on the old boat, and watching the scene develop as we approached. Very soon the men decided it was a smack completely under water, then they counted four people in the rigging, presently one was made out to be a boy; then a little knot of people shewed up on the beach opposite the wreck, and as we got nearer the breeches buoy could be seen at the mast head.

The smack was evidently on the bottom, about a couple of hundred yards from the shore, and as the seas swept across her, she rolled so that the masts described a wide arc across the sky.

But the most tense moment was when we first heard them screaming, or " shrilling " as Sam called it, a most apt description, as those who have heard it will know ; he used to say " when I hear that dreadful shrilling I always know someone is a drowndin'."

A little nearer and we could hear a flood of gibberish, all singing out together. " Why," said some of our folks, " they fare like foreigners ; she's a Johnoh, thass what she is," and then we saw the tug, *Lowestoft*, would be ahead of us, but she dare not go close in like we could, and her crew were getting her lifeboat ready to launch, so we looked like being first alongside, and we were.

Now for the camera. I got a good snap at a little distance, although the light was poor, and the motion pretty wild, then the coxswain sailed her round under the lee of the wreck, and in the midst of lowering sail, getting out oars, throwing grapnel, and general pandemonium, I was able to get a " closeup " of the foremast, and the people hanging on over our heads, half-dressed and wild with excitement ; the boy was astride the forestay, and it was evident he had been there so long he could not move, so the lifeboat was hauled in till she was actually over their deck and right under the crew, and then one of our men went up and helped the boy down.

The other three lost no time sliding down, and then the jabbering broke out again double strength.

We understood, by dint of much bawling, and gesticulating, that one had been landed by the Rocket Brigade, and that then the rope had fouled and the buoy stuck at the mast head and couldn't be moved.

The vessel was a French trawler, the *Joseph et Yvonne* of Dunquerque, with a crew of five; she had struck on the Barnard Sand about four in the morning, the seas had swept her clean over the sand, and she had then drifted and finally sunk a little way from the shore.

The crew had at once taken to the rigging, and had clung there desperately, through the black night, the howling gale, and incessant heavy rolling until they were seen at daylight and the rocket apparatus got to work; then the disappointment when the gear fouled, and relief when the lifeboat was sighted.

When we got away and calmed down a bit, I lined the Frenchmen up and took another snap, and all came out well. Then the *Lowestoft* took our towrope and walked us home at about ten knots; we hoisted our flag to let them know at home we had got the crew, and when we sailed ashore there was the mayor and half the town to give us a cheeroh.

And it was only nine o'clock after all; we had

launched, sailed four miles, got the crew, and towed back. It seemed like half a week, but it was only a crowded hour and a half, while most of England was abed, or just thinking about breakfast.

There was no particular risk to us that day, and I have been on many worse jobs, but there was the fact that at any moment that mast might have gone and the four people drowned; indeed she broke up entirely very soon after we left, and the French Government thought it worthy of recognition, so in 1908 they awarded us all medals and diplomas.

And so my little story ends happily, there were no complaints, and everybody was perfectly satisfied, as the policeman said when the squire died.

My photographs came out in the *Daily Graphic*, then I lent them to the Lifeboat Institution, and not only have I shewn them often myself, but they have been published, and shewn by the Institution all over England; only last year I was presiding at a lifeboat lecture given by a London clergyman, when up came my picture of the *Joseph et Yvonne*, with the crew still hanging there after twenty-six years, but the lecturer had no idea the picture had been taken by his chairman.

I heard the coxswain of the Ramsgate boat give an obviously inspired talk on the wireless, but before they cut him off he got in a little bit of his own, "Amen, thass done, thank God." I wonder! Will my readers say the same?

XXI

A LAST MARDLE AT THE HALF AND HALFER

" O Hollands is a good drink when the nights are
  cold,
  And Brandy is a good drink for them as grows
  old,
  There is lights in the clifftop when the boats
  are homebound,
  And we run the tubs in Suffolk when the word
  goes round."
                    (MR. MASEFIELD, *adapted*).

THERE was subdued excitement at the little inn
one summer evening ; someone had brought in a
copy of a recent *People* with a sensational account
of the twentieth century smuggling trade said to
be carried on by fast motor boats, along the Suffolk
and Essex coasts, and by a coincidence a yacht had
been brought into Eastwick Harbour, which
rumour said was full of stuff.

Toshes was relating how he had been on the
quay when the " Customs Blokes " was rummaging
her, and that he heard there was cases of whisky,
brandy, and cigars, and that he had a yarn with
the skipper, but couldn't make out much except

that she was last from Flushing, and that the owners had gone up to London.

Captain Joe then read out the report in the *People* of a run said to have just been made by a motor boat which met a foreigner, somewhere near the North Hinder Lightship, say fifty miles from our shore, that the stuff had been transhipped, and the cargo landed before daylight, somewhere south of Dunwich, and the general opinion was " There was suffin in it."

Gaffer said there was plenty o' that going on when he was a boy, and the Dutch copers used to do a rare trade with the fishing boats at sea, and a good bit of it got landed this side, but folks didn't put such things in the papers then, and the preventive men were wonderful sharp, and covered the whole coast pretty well every night ; of course, if Government would do away with the " Cosguard " they must expect to have smuggling again.

" Where's that owd stone Betty I give ye Captain ? " said old Gaffer.

" On the top shelf there," said the landlord, pointing to a queer foreign-looking old stone bottle.

" Ah, there she be," said Gaffer, " that belonged to my father that did, and he used to tell me that when he was a youngster, that would be more than a hundred year agoo, about 1820 time I dessay, he was boy aboard of a little coaster called the *Hope*, that used to belong here, a man named Sayers went master of her.

" One time she laid at the quay here, dischargin'
coal, and my father was left aboard alone one night,
as shipkeeper; he was asleep down the foc's'le
when in the middle o' the night he was woke up
by some craft coming alongside, and a lot
people talking and lumping about; he jumps up
on deck, and there was a smugglin' bote just come
in full up with tubs and things.

" Father see a man he knew belonging to Eastwick aboard of her, and the man say ' Goo you
below boy, and don't you see nothin', nor know
nothin', and we'll see that you are paid. So down
he go, and kep' there, but he could hare 'em a
landin' the stuff acrost the *Hope's* decks.

" Then they shoved orf, and must ha' gone up
the river with the rest, 'cos the tub bote was found
the next day mornin' abandoned on the Flats,
them tub botes weren't no vally, made for the
job you know, but they got the stuff away all
right, and none of 'em were catched.

" When father went on deck at daylight time,
there stood that werry identical stone Betty agin
the foc's'le hatch, and that was full o' gin, Dutchman's schnaps you know, and on the quay laid a
lot o' tub slings, what they used to carry the tubs,
tew at a time, one afront, and one behind, with
the slings over the showders; they weighed a
half hund'ed apiece, and the carriers got a guinea
apiece if they got 'em clear all right.

" Well he took them home out 'n the way, but
he must ha' bin seen, 'cos sometime arterwards

the Customs Orficer he come to the house, and axed him where he got them slings. 'Orf the Quay,' my father say, then he wanted to know if father had sin any tubs on the quay; he towd him 'No,' but he di'nt say nothin about the bote, nor the people, nor the Betty o' gin, and there ter be, the werry bottle.

"My owd man he wouldn't ha' parted with that, but I kinder thought that would goo well in the Half an' Halfer, and soo I give it to the Captain here. Father said he heerd the smuggler was a London wassel, but a Suffolk man was master on her, and when he'd sunk his tubs somewhere orf shore, amongst the crabpots on the Ness I dessay, he put into port, and towd the fooks ashore where to goo and creep for 'em.

"'That bote, my father see, must ha' bin and grappled up some o' them tubs and things; I ha' sin the grapplin's they used to work with, the pints were turned round a little way so's the line coont slip out; they were an artful owd crowd them smugglers were, and one o' the Sizewell gang had a little window in the gable of his house where they used to signal to the craft of a night."

"Ah," said the Eelpicker, "I reckon some o' that gin found its way into the Half an' Halfer, and lots o' hard bacca tew; in them days a poor man could get his smook and drink reasonable, but now these here taxes and toteetallers they ruin the country; I could dew with a bit o' hard now I could."

"Dessay," said the landlord, "but this house worn't the Half an' Halfer then, the Ship they used to call it, I've got one of the old licences; Missis, bring me that owd licence paper out of my tin case.

"Look, here ter be, 1764, my word thass more than fifty year afore what Gaffer was a tellin' us; the sign o' the Ship at Eastwick, licence to utter and sell bread and other wittles, beer and ale, but no brandy, rum or Geneva.

"Thass your schnapps, Gaffer; and a certificate of the good fame, sober life and conversation produced accordin' to the Act; ther'ye are together jest you mind your sober life and conversation. All the same I'll lay there's bin some funny owd doin's in this house since that paper was made out, their hids don't ache now what writ that about good fame and sober life."

"Ah, thass true enough," put in Gaffer. "You together racollect owd Jimmy Stanton, whew used to live next doer here fifty yare agoo, him what had that little owd Macaroni schewner, *Try Agin*; he knew suffin about the goin's on on this quay in the owd times, and he could put away a tidy drop hisself when he got a slant. You know Mrs. Stanton was a wunnerful clever owd party, and werry friendly along o' Mrs. Jack Cammell; her husband was master of a bark in the foreign trade. you know, and one day she come into the Bay, and lay dodgin' a bit, time Mrs. Cammell, and owd Jimmy, and his Missis went orf to her from the beach.

" When they got aboard Mrs. Stanton axed the Captain to let the min sail her orf into the sea a bit, and put her round a time or tew, so as she might see how they tacked a square rigged wassel, so he give the order to the mate, and then he and owd Jimmy went below, and had saveral drops.

" By'n bye they reached in agin, and that was time to goo ashore, and when owd Jimmy come on deck he was a little bit tiddley, hows'ever he gets down into the bote all right, but when they got ashore he was wuss, and as sune as he got out o' the bote, down he goo lump on to the beach.

" ' Oh dear, Oh dear,' say his Missis, ' look Mr. Stanton is took bad, run quick, Sam,' she says, ' up to the Jolly Sailor, and get him a drop o' brandy,' soo up goo Sam, though iverybody, 'ceptin' the owd gal, could see what was a matter, and comes back with a glass o' brandy, and blow me if that dint pull the owd chap together for a minute, and he says ' Whoop Mrs. Shtanton, what a day we are havin', I'll give ye a Suffolk toast,' he say.

" ' Here's to my wife's husband," and with that down goo the rest o' the brandy, and down goo Jimmy, and they had to carry him home."

" Poor owd Jimmy Stanton," says the landlord, " but I was really thinking of them owd war times when Boney used to help the smugglers over the tother side for the money and information they used to take across, and there was plenty of money for them this side too, and they spent it free.

" The stuff used to be stowed away under ground in all sorts o' out o' the way places, and I've heard tell of smugglers holds all along o' the coast, Bawdsey, Orford, Aldebro, Sizewell, Dunwich, Westleton, Southwold, Benacre, right as far as Yarmouth.

" The beach yolls used to go right across to Flushing them times to fetch the tubs, and they were a daring lot them Yarmouth chaps, there worn't much could catch a yoll unless they got an onlucky shot into them ; and they used to build 'em up to sixty foot I've heard, and more, open boats, and they'd carry a saw to cut through the thwarts if they were chased, 'cos the boats sailed faster so ; I recollect one they called the owd *Errywiggle*, on account o' her working so much when they pressed her regattaring.

" I once read a piece in a paper about a Yarmouth yoll called the *Aboukir Belle*, about 1800 time, that said she was eighty foot long, and nothin' cont catch her, and carried a gun too.

" Well, one night she was chased by a cutter in the Roads, and the smugglers fired and shot the cutter's mast away, so she drove ashore, and the crew looked like bein' washed out of her, but they let go an anchor and wore the yoll down to the wreck, and took all the preventives out of her.

" Then they broarched a tub o' Hollands, and all had a good drink together, and through savin' the people like that the smugglers went clear all alright, though the yoll was chock full o' contraband.

" Them Yarmouth Blowters were a tough lot, and the Rows were full o' hides for ' Moonshine.' An owd gal, what died there a few years back, over ninety, she towd me once she could recollect bein' scared hearin' the smugglers runnin' past of a night, and that they used a public house in one of the Rows what had so many back ways into other Rows, and hidin' holes, that they were never catched there, nor none of the smuggled goods nayther.

" But them days is gone now, and if smugglin' dew come up agin that'll be regular dukes, with fast motor yachts, and motor cars, like them rum runners in Americky, and little people on't have no chance.

" They did say that little steam yacht what used to come trawling about here, and belonged up o' the Broads somewhere, was up to that game ; owd Smoker went master of her one time, but he won't know nothin' about such work.

" I say though, look at the clock, we shall have the pleeceman here directly if I keep on a mardlin' like this. So drink up together, and I'll give ye a last toast :

" ' Here's to them as has old clothes and no one to mend 'em ; Damn them as has thousands o' pounds and no heart to spend 'em.' "

GLOSSARY OF SUFFOLK WORDS USED

AGIN.—Against.
ALLUS.—Always.
ARIDDY.—Already.
ARTICLE.—A queer customer.
AXE.—Ask.

BACKUS.—The Backhouse (Scullery).
BARDSNAZIN.—Bird's nesting.
BOR.—Short for neighbour.
BRUCE's TIME.—Mr. Bruce, M.P., promoted the Closing Act
for public houses.

CHERRY-MERRY.—Slightly the better for drink.
CLOSE.—Clothes.
CLOUT.—To strike.
CUPPY WHEY.—Word for turning a horse to the left.

DAVILTRY.—Devilry.
DEW.—Do.
DICKEY.—Donkey.
DRAT, DROT.—Abbreviation of God rot.
DREEPIN.—Dripping.
DUDDER. To tremble with cold, or fright.
DUZZY.—Muddle headed.

ENOW.—Enough.
ERRYWIGGLE.—Earwig.
FARE.—Seem.
FILD.—Field.
FO'T.—For it.

FLYING HOSS.—Pegasus.
FRAP.—A muddle.
FUDDER.—Further.
FULFER.—Fieldfare.

GIN or GON.—Give—Gave.
GOOF.—Corn stacked in a barn.
GOTCH.—Jug.
GRET.—Great.

HALF AND HALFER.—Fishing boat where owner and crew went
     halves.
HEFTY.—Unsettled.
HIDE.—To beat.
HOPE.—To help.
HOLL.—A dry ditch.
HORNIPIES.—Peewits.
HOSS-OILS.—Elliman's Embrocation.
HULL.—To throw.
HULVER.—Holly.

INNARDS.—One's inside.

JOHNOH.—A Frenchman, or Belgian.
JUGGLE.—To nestle up like partridges at night.

KILLER.—A small open tub.
KINDLIN.—Sticks for fire lighting.
KING HARRY.—Goldfinch.

LESS.—Let us.

MACARONI.—A fore and aft schooner with no foretopmast.
MANDER.—Manner.
MARN'T.—May not.
MARDLE.—A gossip, to yarn.
MASTER.—Wonderful.
MAVISH.—Thrush.
MEESE.—Mice.
MOB.—To chaff.
MOONSHINE.—Smuggled spirits.

Nothe.—North.

Offspring.—An illegitimate.

Piece o' Paper.—A summons, usually of the police court variety.
Pightle.—The little man's little field.
Polterin.—Seeking for oddments along the sea-shore.
Puny.—Piano in early days.

Rockalow.—Bad weather coat (Roquelaure, Tristram Shandy).
Roke.—Sea-fog.
Ruff.—Roof.

Shock.—Sheaves of corn stood up in a field.
Shod.—Shed.
Showders.—Shoulders.
Shruck.—Shrieked.
Shue.—Shewed.
Shuff.—Shove.
Shugg.—Shake.
Shummaker.—Shoemaker.
Silly-Bold.—An over free and impertinent child.
Slammakin.—An awkward, gawky girl.
Snaasty.—Disagreeable.
Soshways.—On the slant.
Stammed.—Astonished.
Suffin.—Something.

Tew.—To, too, towed.
Thass.—That is.
Throshold.—Threshold.
Titter ma Tatter.—See Saw.
Together.—Persons gathered together.
Tother.—The other.
Treakle.—Trickle.
Tree.—Three.
Trosh.—Thrash.

Waate.—Wheat.
Whoyeesh.—Word for turning a horse to the right.

WIPER.—Viper.
WITTLES.—Victuals.
WOYAGES.—Fishing voyages.
WROWT.—Worked, wrought.

YOLL.—Beach yawl.